FREELANCING IN TOKYO
(Revised & Updated)

A Unique Guide to Achieving Financial Success in Japan's Most Expensive City

DAVID CHESTER

Shining Hour Publishing

FREELANCING IN TOKYO

(November 2015)

Published by

Shining Hour Publishing

For more information, visit *www.freelancingintokyo@com*

Cover design by Alex Saavedra

Cover photo by Jürgen Stack

(Photo description: "Young women in Roppongi's new shopping and expat living area, Roppongi Hills.")

ISBN 978-0-9839981-1-2

ACKNOWLEDGMENTS

I gratefully acknowledge the time and talents of Terry Wolverton, William Tyree and Michelle Dalton Tyree, Ritsuko Arisaka, and Tracy Burns. Their input, advice, encouragement and friendship helped me write *Freelancing in Tokyo* with a sense of confidence and purpose.

I also wish to thank…

Blake Pinter and Kimberly Tierney for being constant sources of inspiration,

Colleen Sakurai for her friendship, for giving me a place to stay when I first arrived in Japan and for teaching me that "Big money comes easy; small money comes hard,"

Ellen Sandler for teaching and inspiring me,

Greg Irwin for being a great friend, for all the great jobs (and greater stories) and for helping me (try to) understand Japan,

Marc and Sherri Nussbaum for their lifelong friendship and for believing in my creative abilities,

Marsha Span for being a friend, mentor and the first person to encourage me to write,

Matthew Dandurand, Alejandro Saavedra and Luke Swenson for their creative visions,

Robin Hosmer Erenberg for her friendship and support,

Ryan Hawkins for helping me keep my head above water,

Wendy Silverman Tobiska for her lifelong friendship and for being a beacon of truth and honesty,

My family and friends, both in the United States and Japan, who have supported me emotionally through the years, and…

Minoru, who pulled back the curtains and let the sunlight in.

This book is dedicated to the memory of

my beloved parents, Albert and Maxine Chester, who always believed in me, even if I didn't believe in myself,

and

my best friend, Marc Reiss, who was more brilliant and beautiful than he ever knew,

and

Donald Richie, who inspired me in ways that I was never able to tell him. Thank you, Mr. Richie, for all the rich, finely-detailed observations of the Japan I really wanted to know, but was born too late to. Through your wonderful books and words, I was able to "see" a magical world that once was.

CONTENTS

First journal entry upon arriving in Tokyo:

April 1, 1993

First reaction: Twilight Zone meets Disneyland meets Manhattan.

Most recent journal entry prior to publication of this book:

November 1, 2015

Still not sure I understand anything about Japan, but I'm a bit more comfortable than I was when I first arrived.

WHY FREELANCE IN TOKYO?

Your questions answered

Isn't Tokyo one of the most expensive cities in the world? Isn't it crowded? Isn't it difficult for non-Japanese to deal with the customs, language and Byzantine rules and regulations?

In a word, yes. On the other hand, Tokyo has so much to offer on so many levels that it can be the most exciting, thrilling roller coast ride you've ever taken. Think of it as Disneyland-meets-Twilight Zone set in a safer New York City: You can't help but be entertained and mystified at the same time. Also, as Tokyo is much more of a global city than you might imagine, it is guaranteed you will work with and/or befriend people from around the world, automatically expanding your cultural horizons and imbuing you with a level of sophistication and worldliness (or enhancing the level you already have). Most importantly, as a "stranger in a strange land," you will discover Tokyo offers a world of freelance job opportunities you might not have otherwise considered: actor, chef, model, teacher, voiceover artist and more. What's particularly great about these jobs is you can get hired to do the majority of them *without having special training or skills,* with a starting salary that will almost certainly be anywhere from US$30-150 an hour. Compare those numbers with what you can get in your own country for doing similar jobs (*with* proper training) and Tokyo will start to look quite attractive.

Consider these October 2013 statistics from Japan's Ministry of Health, Labor and Welfare (the most recent at time of publishing): The number of foreign workers employed in Japan "stood at 717,504." That is almost 1.5 times higher than the number available when *FIT* was first published in 2009. Also, as with previous years, the highest concentration of foreign workers is in Tokyo. True, there is no specific mention foreign freelance workers, but the numbers are a clear indication that enough foreigners still think Japan, and specifically Tokyo, has enough to offer in the job arena that they are willing to uproot their lives and make a go of it here.

That is exactly what I did: In 1993, after being given the opportunity to write songs for an American girl group that was popular in Japan, I decided to see if I could find success in the Japanese music business. With a few thousand dollars, a three-month tourist visa and the promise of a floor to sleep on in Tokyo, I packed up and left my hometown of Los Angeles.

At first I thought I had made a terrible mistake. The Japanese pop music business did open its doors—but only wide enough to offer me coffee and meetings with English-speaking staff who listened politely while I tried to convince them of my value.

This led nowhere fast. I could see any number of professionally dressed Westerners in Tokyo marching off to their prospective futures. These people weren't tourists; what did they know that I didn't? A lot more than I ever would, I imagined. My Japanese skills were negligible, I had no college degree, I was relatively clueless about life and money, and my practical work experience was spotty at best. And yet… within eight months of arriving in Tokyo, I had scored a brand new *manshon* (Western-style apartment), was living a fantastic new life with friends, dates and fun, and was earning as much as US$7,000 a month—all from well-paying freelance positions.

How did I do that? By learning the power of the *meishi* (business card). Remember: In 1993, when I arrived, I did not have the advantages of the Internet or a smartphone. But I did have a *meishi* (more on this later). Although some people may consider it to be quaint or even passé, the simple, elegant act of exchanging *meishi* in Japan is still a powerful network-building tool. By exchanging *meishi* with everyone I met and letting them know I was seeking work (of any kind), job offers soon started pouring in. And what I discovered was: *every* skill I had ever learned (or half-way learned), from writing business letters to tap dancing (!), was suddenly a valuable commodity in Tokyo. More importantly, I took *every* job offered, even ones I didn't think I could do ("Be a French chef for a day? Sure, no problem!"), and never looked back. In just over three years I had saved a substantial amount of money, at which point I was living in a brand new condo with a loving Japanese partner, playing piano at Tokyo's top hotels, and had appeared on the cover of a national Japanese men's health magazine (the issue was focused on hair—I was the "no-hair" model). I was also acting in commercials with big name Japanese stars, doing character voices for video games and, yes, teaching English—at major Japanese corporations. ALL these were freelance jobs.

However, before you jump on the next plane to Japan (or even if you already have), having insights into living/working in Tokyo will put you ahead of the crowd. This, then, is the purpose of *Freelancing in Tokyo (FIT)*: to provide you with what you need to know to have a successful career as a freelancer in Tokyo. If you follow the advice offered in *FIT* and are truly willing to put in the effort, there is no reason why you can't earn US$50-75K within your first year.

FIT is ideal for native English speakers and is best suited for the reader who has at least a B.A. (or equivalent), some work experience (in any field), basic Japanese (i.e. being able to greet others, introduce yourself and ask for assistance; also see "Japanese 101"), and who currently holds a proper visa to work legally in Japan or has the means to obtain one. For more information on these matters, see "Making the Decision" and "Getting Set Up."

FIT also has value for spouses of people who have relocated to Tokyo for job assignments, for students (who can only work part-time jobs because of visa restrictions), and even for individuals who have been in Tokyo for several years working "regular" jobs, unsure of how to earn extra yen.

While reams have been written about living/working in Tokyo (and Japan), what makes *FIT* unique is that all job descriptions (except "Host/Hostess," and "Waitstaff") are based on my first-hand experience. In addition, the *FIT* website (*freelancingintokyo.com*) features sound files for all the essential phrases (§ "Helpful Phrases") listed in *FIT*, as well as extensive lists of valuable links (all categorized) to assist you in your freelance adventure.

To ease your transition from tourist to freelancing professional, I suggest first reading "Making the Decision" and "Getting Set Up." If you've already passed those two hurdles, you can head straight for "Jobs." For all readers, "Things You Should Know" offers some tips, wit and wisdom gleaned from my years of freelancing in Tokyo.

Note: Except for quoted commentary contained in the "Jobs" chapter, *FIT* is based on my personal experiences in Tokyo as a freelance actor, entertainer, journalist, screenwriter, songwriter, teacher and voiceover artist. Some readers may observe that in the midst of those experiences I comment on food, food prices, personal space and noise levels, as well as other things that may not directly relate to freelancing. I do, but I feel it is important to include this commentary as some people are very sensitive to noise, some have food issues and others may not fully understand how limited space truly is in Tokyo (and Japan). The reader's own freelancing experience may be completely different than mine.

❖

ROAD MAP

Japanese words, webdings and money

Instead of repeating certain items throughout *FIT*, I've listed them here for quick reference.

Japanese words

- Except for dialogues in the "Helpful Phrases" section, each Japanese word in the text first appear as follows: the romanized version of the Japanese word (according to the Hepburn system of romanization, or *rōmaji* in Japanese), followed by its English equivalent in parentheses.

- I frequently refer to the three "alphabets" (character sets) used to write the Japanese language: *kanji* (multistroke characters borrowed from the Chinese language, used extensively in Japanese verbs); *hiragana* (a cursive script for simplified *kanji*, grammatical words and inflections); and *katakana* (an angular script usually reserved for foreign loan words and emphasis). *Hiragana* and *katakana* charts can be found in "Japanese 101."

Webdings, etc.

- Recorded phrases available on the *FIT* website are referenced in the text by: (👂)

- Links available on the *FIT* website are referenced in the text by: (🔗)

- When referring to anything that needs to be translated to/from either Japanese or English, you may see J-E or E-J.

Money

All monetary figures presented in the text are in Japanese yen (marked with the yen symbol, ¥). As exchange rates fluctuate daily it is not realistic to list U.S. dollar equivalents. For reference keep a calculator handy or bookmark your favorite currency calculator (📎 "Exchange Rates").

If you are unfamiliar with Japanese money you may see numbers that that look like huge amounts; they aren't. An easy way to understand the yen/U.S. dollar ratio is to drop the last two zeros of any Japanese monetary figure (i.e. if you drop the last two zeros of ¥25,000, you have US$250). This is a *very rough* conversion and only provided for a quick example. Exchange rates change often and it's incumbent upon you to check them often. At some point you will have (hopefully) saved a large amount of yen. Avoid the temptation to send money home every month and try instead to catch a "good wave" when the rates are in your favor. The difference can be anywhere between several hundred and several thousand (U.S.) dollars.

❖

MAKING THE DECISION

Saying goodbye… and saying hello

Coming to Tokyo, setting up an apartment and finding gainful employment has been one of the best adventures of my life. Still, even with the amount of research and planning I did, there was much I was unprepared for. Following are steps you can take, prior to your move, so you can feel in control of your destiny as a freelancer in Tokyo.

Make FIT your new best friend

Shameless promotion? Perhaps. On the other hand, having the e-version of *FIT* on your tablet or smartphone allows you to quickly access advice, keywords and phrases that can benefit you while you're out and about.

Explore the FIT website (freelancingintokyo.com)

As mentioned, the *FIT* website includes hundreds of links to valuable websites, organized by category (§ "Helpful Websites"). It will hopefully provide novices and "experts" alike with essential information for a successful freelancing life in Tokyo.

Know Your Basic Japanese!

In classified ads found in Japan's English-language daily newspapers (see § "Media") you will often see: "fluency in Japanese a must," "must be able to speak, read and write Japanese," and phrases of this nature. Some of these ads blatantly state: "Japanese (nationals) only." What does this mean for you? If your skills are highly specialized, you may be able to come to Japan without speaking Japanese, land a plum job and make tons of money. If not, you will quickly be relegated to jobs not requiring Japanese: teaching English and/or positions requiring native English speakers. However, it is *not* essential to speak Japanese to make an excellent living in Tokyo. In fact, sometimes the Japanese prefer if you *don't* speak their language.

This enables them to help you as you flounder about. On the other hand, why limit yourself? Look beyond jobs for which the only requirement is to be a native English speaker. Arrive computer-literate, with a college degree and the ability to speak, read and write basic Japanese—which you can do by learning the relatively simple *hiragana* characters (there are less than 100), and *katakana* characters (variations of the *hiragana*), not the 2,000 multistroke *kanji* required to read a Japanese newspaper.

For those with little to no knowledge of the Japanese language, I have included a *hiragana* and *katakana* chart, as well as basic phrases you can use from day one in Tokyo (see "Japanese 101"). For those with a stronger grasp of Japanese, the sooner you familiarize yourself with *FIT*'s "Helpful Phrases," the sooner you can navigate through the challenging situations you are sure to encounter during your *FIT* experience.

Start Exercising (if You Haven't Already)

Despite vast improvements in the subway/train stations (i.e. the addition of escalators and elevators), unless you are wealthy enough to take taxis everywhere, you will be doing *lots* of walking in Tokyo, if not running. If you're used to doing that already, great; if you aren't, start an exercise program immediately. If you are already in Tokyo, there are any number of *gaijin* (foreigner)-friendly sports clubs (see § "Fitness"), several with English-speaking staff and trainers.

Check Out Tokyo On a Tourist Visa

While others who have experienced Tokyo may disagree, it is my belief that *before* you make any long-term goals to live/work in Tokyo, *first* come on a tourist visa and give it a good once-over. This requires an additional investment, but an invaluable one.

Most Western countries, including the United States, issue a 90-day tourist visa to Japan, giving you ample time to observe Tokyo up close. You can set yourself up in an affordable monthly apartment (see both "Getting Set Up: Accommodations" and § "Accommodations"), hang out with fellow foreigners (and grill them for valuable info), scope out areas you might like to live, experience Japan's amazingly punctual transportation system and get over the shock of the high food prices. Also, this would be a great time to meet potential employers. (If you're ready to take things a step further, see "Getting Set Up: Visa Sponsors.")

Next, find a quiet place to reflect on your time here. Are you ready to embrace another world, have an adventure, and spend two or more years of your life here? Great, go for it—but *first* make a list of clearly defined goals. If you don't, you will quickly become sucked into Tokyo's frantic pace; with all the opportunities and stimuli, you may forget your reasons for coming in the first place. Here are some suggestions:

- To become fluent in Japanese with an eye toward interpreting for celebrities, major corporations, etc.

- To start your own business

- To earn enough to buy a piece of property

- To save _____ (amount of money) by _____ (date)

- To gain additional skills to apply to a future career

I learned the hard way that having clearly-defined goals for your Tokyo life helps you avoid panicked moments when you find yourself lost on some tiny street, surrounded by wooden houses, skyscrapers, Buddhist temples (or massage parlors) asking, "Why am I here?"

Of course, your goals might change; *you* might change. But promise me before you roll out the *futon* (Japanese bedding), *have a goal.*

So, assuming goals are in order (or soon will be), now's the time to turn the page and get set up for your exciting Tokyo life.

❖

GETTING SET UP

Visas and Accommodations

Getting a work visa and finding a place to live are your biggest hurdles in Tokyo. Lessen them by familiarizing yourself with the vast resources about living/working in Japan available on the Internet (including the *FIT* website). Meanwhile, here are some tips to keep in mind before proceeding.

Visas

Rules allowing foreigners to work in another country may change at any time, so the following is provided as a basic overview. As of this writing, Japan has seven types of visas (§ "Immigration/Visas"). You will need to obtain one of them to work here legally. Unless you have a student visa, or dependent visa (meaning you are married to a foreigner who is legally working in Japan), both which allow you to work a limited number of hours per week, what you need to obtain a proper work visa is: a legitimate college degree, verifiable certification or 10 years of working experience in a specific field that can be easily applied in Japan (i.e. teaching English as a second language, interpreter/translator, etc.), and, most importantly, a *hoshōnin* (visa sponsor; see below).

Without the degree or certificate, you *may* be able to get a visa, but essentially you are courting trouble and creating frustration for yourself. I learned this firsthand when I tried to get a work visa with only a certificate from a music school and a résumé that listed several years of work experience. Without the help of my visa sponsor going to bat for me and convincing the immigration authorities I was a valuable asset to his office, there would be no *FIT*. So, while there are exceptions to the rules, having a legitimate degree makes obtaining your work visa much easier.

Visa Sponsors

Whether you have a diploma or certificate, neither have value without a visa sponsor. A visa sponsor can be a company or individual that satisfies certain conditions set by the Japanese Immigration Bureau. Some of these require the visa sponsor to divulge information about his/her financial status and/or business. Not everyone is willing to do this; however, if a company or an individual's business is a legitimate one, this condition should not pose a problem.

How do you find this magical company/individual? This is part of your adventure and ultimately the key to your success in Tokyo. Internet research may help you find a Japanese company willing to sponsor you because it requires your unique skills (such companies often include English language schools). If this is the case you might be able to secure a work visa *before* coming to Japan, enabling you to arrive with the proper documents (and, most likely, with accommodations waiting) and hit the ground running. This is the ideal situation—although you might end up doing a job you don't like just to have gotten "in." You might also be able to land a visa sponsor by registering with websites (see § "Jobs") that feature jobs in Japan; however, employers that use these sites to recruit new employees are unlikely to sponsor you unless you are physically *in* Japan. (Yes, it can be a Catch-22 situation.)

While the above methods might help you obtain a visa sponsor, keep in mind you will most likely have to work fulltime for that sponsor. In the case of some language schools, "fulltime" might be advertised as "25 hours a week." This doesn't mean you are footloose and fancy-free the rest of the time (see "Jobs: Teaching English, Salary"). Generally, your schedule will be controlled in such a way that it will *not* allow you to do any of the other great jobs listed in *FIT*—jobs which can help you achieve financial success.

The solution is to find an understanding sponsor who is either willing to hire you in name only, or only requires a limited amount of your workweek. This type of situation is more common than you might imagine.

Find Your "Dream Sponsor"

To find your "dream sponsor" I suggest first coming to Tokyo on a tourist visa (see "Making the Decision"). Being the savvy individual you are, you will have arrived armed with a J-E résumé, a J-E *meishi* (that features your face photo) and a smartphone. As soon as you are able, set yourself up in a monthly apartment (see this chapter) and start networking.

If you are not yet in Tokyo, start researching the links available on the *FIT* website, send out your query emails and have meetings lined up for when you arrive. While this "pre-networking" has some value, the fastest route to a visa sponsor and work visa in Tokyo is being *physically present*. Also:

- Attend events where fellow Westerners gather. Listings for these events can be found on social networking sites that you may already be using, and in English-language media such as *The Japan Times, Mainichi Daily News* and *Daily Yomiuri*; see § "Media"). Have your *meishi* with you and don't be shy about handing it out. Tell people you are qualified in such-and-such a field and that you are seeking a visa sponsor. (You may find people unwilling to give up their contacts, but someone is always ready to help a newbie, so speak up!)

- Start collecting other people's *meishi*. Send "nice to have met you" emails or "I'll be here for one more month and I'd appreciate a meeting" emails—whatever is required to maintain your newfound contacts. As your circle expands, remind everyone you are actively seeking work and would be appreciative of any other contacts they might have. By "working" your collection of *meishi* in a gentle, but persistent way you will be opening doors to a long list of additional contacts, one whom might become your visa sponsor.

- The "English language school" route to getting a work visa is sometimes the easiest; I have much more to say on this topic later, but for now, if you feel this is the right path for you, try this: In addition to answering the plethora of ads found on almost every "jobs-in-Japan" website (see § "Employment Opportunities"), boldly walk into any language school you see and announce you are looking for work. If you are dressed professionally and have your résumé with you, you might be offered a job on the spot (providing the company is willing to sponsor you).

The above is a short list of suggestions to help you land a visa sponsor. Every Westerner I met in Tokyo had their own story about how they obtained theirs. Even if you start by working at an English language school, ultimately you should be able to find a company/individual to sponsor you, one that does not necessarily require you to work for them. For example: The visa sponsor may become one in name only (meaning you might be required to show up on the odd day and/or are now free to work for whoever you please). Alternatively, once you are able to string together enough *steady* freelance (part-time) jobs from which you earn a salary of approximately ¥250,000 a month, you can (in most cases) then sponsor *yourself*. This requires you to show Japanese immigration authorities your income statements, contract letters and possibly year-end tax statements as well (see § "Self-sponsorship"). I repeat, you must *first* be sponsored by a company/individual in Japan (for a reasonable time, probably as long as a year) before you can sponsor yourself.

Meanwhile, when you have found someone to be your sponsor, you/your sponsor must contact the local immigration bureau to obtain your application and any other paperwork required to process your visa (§ "Immigration/Visas"). Once you have submitted the paperwork, which must include a copy of your college diploma and/or certificate indicating your proficiency in some technical/vocational skill, the likelihood of your work visa being approved is relatively high. (Note: Make sure you have the *originals* of these documents in case you are asked for them.)

On the off chance your application is not approved, don't despair: You can return on another 90-day tourist visa and try again, or try to get a student visa, if you are so inclined. (One way to do this is through a language school, although not all language schools offer visas; see § "Japanese Language Schools.") From my survey of a cross-section of Americans and Canadians of different age groups and technical backgrounds, most obtained their work visas within a three-month period of time. So, don't obsess over this part—once the right documents have been processed, you should be sitting pretty.

Once you have obtained your work visa, your next concern is...

Accommodations (§ "Accommodations")

Because of the Internet, finding a temporary/permanent place to live in Tokyo is no longer filled with the anxiety foreigners faced in the past. You can easily find websites, in English, with incredibly detailed information that address all your concerns, as well as online ads for used furniture, electronics and appliances. Why buy used? With the flux of people leaving Tokyo after short-term assignments, you're sure to find quality used items to furnish your new *apāto* ("Japanese-style" apartment) or *manshon* ("Western-style" apartment).

As to whether to choose an *apāto* or *manshon,* keep the following in mind: *Apāto* are in older buildings, often have *tatami* (straw mat) floors, *shoji* (sliding wooden doors with paper frames) for dividing rooms, a kitchenette with a *gasu tēburu* ("gas table," a one- or two-ring gas range), a Japanese bath (but no shower), a Japanese-style squat toilet (although some have Western-style ones), and walls so thin you can hear your neighbors snoring (or shagging). *Manshon,* on the other hand, are almost always in newer buildings, have hardwood floors (or floors that look like they're hardwood), Western-style sit-down toilets and walls which *may* be thicker. *Manshon* are usually more expensive than *apāto,* but, as I know you will be successful in Tokyo, pay a little more so you can live in a presentable place and be comfortable. Some may choose to have the "Japanese" experience—and walking across a cool *tatami* mat floor in the summer can be a treat—but in my experience living in a *manshon* is better overall (and more impressive to potential students/clients, if you decide to work from home).

As with any other metropolis, location is more important than the quality of your new Tokyo digs. Do not consider this lightly. Imagine: You find a clean space ("space" more accurately describes the living quarters most newbies—or, in fact, anyone in Tokyo—can afford) off the beaten track, a mere 15-minute walk from the nearest subway/train station. You say, "I can walk. The exercise will do me good." Yes, if you are training for a marathon, it will. But after a 16-hour day running ragged across town, juggling up to four freelance jobs, you will quickly resent that 15-minute trek.

To avoid this: 1) research monthly apartments and guest-houses in Tokyo (§ "Accommodations"); or 2) come to Tokyo on a tourist visa to find *exactly* what area you might want to live in. Wherever that is, *make sure it's central*. Central means anywhere near one of the following major subway and/or train stations: Akasaka-Mitsuke, Ginza, Ikebukuro, Ogikubo, Shinjuku, Shibuya or Tokyo.

You will also want to live near the above-named stations because that's where most major businesses (and hence jobs) are located. When I say "near," I mean not more than a 5-10 minute walk to the station; at the end of the day you will be glad you took my advice.

Familiarize yourself with these stations and surrounding areas in advance by downloading any one of the many apps for the Tokyo metro/subway/train system or by purchasing similar guides or maps (see § "Tokyo Subways/Trains"). If you are unsure how to say the station names, take a Japanese lesson to learn them and any other vocabulary related to subway/train transportation.

Other things to consider:

- Is there a good supermarket near where you want to live (not just 24/7 convenience stores)? Do *not* underestimate this or you will be eating *bentō bako* (lunch boxes) every day. If that's your idea of haute cuisine, *dōzo* (go ahead).

- Is there a park or nature area within walking distance? Do not underestimate this either, unless you enjoy being surrounded 24/7 by concrete and steel.

- Is the building you want to live in off the main street? If not, not only will you hear/smell the traffic, but at bed-time you will also enjoy the enchanting sounds of the *bōsōzoku* (motorcycle gangs) ripping down the boulevards, revvin' their bikes to wake the dead.

- Is there a *koin randorī* (Laundromat) nearby or space in the apartment for a washing machine? (Very important! See "Laundry" in "Things You Should Know.")

Let's say you've found a nice place to live. Before calling a moving company, be aware that the following businesses can be conducted near residential areas, not to mention *in* residential buildings:

- *shingakujuku* (or *juku*): private after-school classes (also known as "cram school") where students study to help pass exams to enter institutions of higher learning;

- *sunakku bā* ("snack bar"): a bar that serves pricey drinks and "snacks" (crackers, dried squid or *tsukemono* [pickled vegetables]);

- *hosutesu kurabu* ("hostess club"): overpriced clubs, some as small as large walk-in closets, where men chat with pretty women (Japanese/foreign) who light their cigarettes and pour their drinks;

- *rabu hoteru*: love hotel (see § "Love Hotels");

- *massāji* (massage) or *sōpurando* ("soapland"): establishments where men are "massaged" or "bathed" by young women;

- *pachinko* parlor: a gambling establishment; and

- "live" clubs: nightclubs

These types of businesses may appeal to some, but for others the disadvantages can include noise, loitering, neon lights, etc. One last caveat: Take a gander out your new apartment window *before* signing a lease, just in case there happens to be a *cemetery* in joss stick-tossing distance. This might not bother some; others may not enjoy the "view" of Grandma Hiroko's final resting place.

If there are any zoning laws in Tokyo, I have never seen any in action. People open up their businesses wherever they please. If you happen to be living next to someone who is running a "massage" business out of their apartment, unless you own the apartment building, your options are limited. This definitely is *not* a standard situation. I've never experienced it in the four places I've lived in Tokyo, but I've seen it—and so will you.

Also, before laying down your lifesavings to move in (see later this chapter), stroll through your new neighborhood on a

Saturday or Sunday. Make *absolutely sure* there is no music being pumped into the streets from the loudspeakers located on telephone poles—poles that lean precariously close to the apartment building you are thinking of moving into. (See "Music in the Streets" in "Things You Should Know.")

All right: You've found the area, the building, the apartment. Now make sure you are crystal clear on the following:

Unless you are staying in some sort of temporary guesthouse specifically for foreigners, you are again required to have a *hoshōnin* ("sponsor" but in this case, "guarantor") to help you secure the apartment of your dreams. This is unavoidable and some Japanese have to do it, too (especially students or those who cannot show proof of employment).

Finding a guarantor need not be a Herculean undertaking. Guarantors can be employers, Japanese friends or Japanese spouses. However, they, like visa sponsors, may be required to divulge enough information about their financial status to prove to the *fudōsangyōsha* (real estate agent) that they could cover any costs (i.e. back rent) if you were to suddenly skip the country.

Most Westerners I know have not had difficulty finding a guarantor, but if you don't find one right away, don't panic. Worst-case scenario: Rent a monthly, furnished apartment from agencies that do not require guarantors. These apartments are in fact the *manshon*-type apartments mentioned earlier, but usually a bit smaller. (See § "Accommodations")

Meanwhile, remember two things: 1) Japanese landlords and real estate agencies feel if a guarantor is willing to be held financially responsible for you, they (the landlords/agencies) are willing to let you live on their property; and 2) foreigners are held to a higher standard of behavior, period. So, as the intelligent and responsible adult you are, promise me this: If a Japanese person has gone out of his/her way to help you, don't screw it up by being late with the rent, having loud parties or causing problems in the building. If this is the type of person you are, don't come up to me on the street saying, "I got kicked out of my new *manshon* because I blasted my stereo till 3:00 a.m." Even if you are *perfect*, the Japanese will be judging you (as long as you are living here, I might add). Be respectful of the situation and, hopefully, you will be respected in kind.

More importantly, in order to get *in* to your new pad, you will most likely be required to pay:

- *yachin* (rent): first and last month;
- *shikikin* (security deposit): usually an amount equivalent to one or two months of rent to cover any "damages" (you may receive some of this back if the apartment is in *perfect* condition, but not necessarily; regardless, take before/after pictures!);
- *reikin* ("key money"/reward/gift): usually two or *three* months rent; considered a "gift" to the *ooya* (landlord);
- *chūkai tesūryō*: a commission of one-month rent paid to the real estate agent, assuming you have used one.

If you consider a decent place will cost anywhere between ¥85,000-120,000 a month, and that you may have to pay up to seven months of rent money in *advance*... do the math. Insane? Yes. Paying "key money" is not as prevalent as it once was—but unless you have a lawyer, Japanese spouse or connections to some higher authority (God would be nice), you will most likely be contributing to the landlord's college trust fund for his/her grandchildren.

Shocked? Good. This will be one of many you will experience if you decide to make Tokyo your home. I looked at it this way: If other people had come here and made fortunes, so could I. I swallowed hard, paid the money and never thought about it again. I made it all back in two months because I quickly discovered what was available to me as a freelancer—as you will if you keep reading.

❖

JOBS

Big money comes easy; small money comes hard.

Assuming you have or will have a visa that allows you to legally work in Japan (see "Getting Set Up"), you are ready to add to your existing income or start earning a nice living as a freelancer. Some general notes before we start:

- As mentioned in "Why Freelance in Tokyo?", keep a calculator or currency converter handy to calculate the current exchange rate for yen amounts listed in the text.

- Check the *FIT* website regularly (*freelancingintokyo.com*) for valuable links to job sites and more. Register with these sites, get on their e-mail lists and check in often.

- Get networking. Hand out your J-E *meishi* and tell everyone that you teach, write, edit, act and do voice work (even if you never have). You should be able to earn an *additional* ¥500,000 to ¥2 million a year as a freelancer, separate from other "regular" work you may find.

- If you see classified ads on Tokyo's English-language sites (see § "Media") that do not mention a specific salary, think twice before contacting them. While most ads state salaries, those that don't are often for positions that require technical skills (and for which salaries will be negotiated) or for positions offered by companies that ask you to come in for an interview, only to tell you the hourly rate is between ¥2,000-3,300. That might sound like good money at first, but there are *hundreds* of these "opportunities" (English teaching, proofreading, etc.)—all which pay exactly the same. You can get higher hourly salaries on your own, as you will soon learn. In the meantime: If you see "editor/writer needed for a global management consulting firm" with no mention of salary,

I'd say it's safe to assume a reasonable salary might be offered. But if you see "cheerful, energetic head teacher needed for a children's English school, just an express train ride away from Shinjuku"* with no mention of salary, don't waste your time—because that's what you'll be doing.

* Shinjuku is a major subway / train station in Tokyo.

- Interviews are sometimes done in groups. It won't happen often, but when it does, be prepared to find yourself in a room with an interviewer and five other job candidates.

- If you take a full-time position teaching English at a language school, many companies pay a starting salary of ¥250,000 per month. (Note: "full-time" for language schools generally means 20-25 hours per week.) This salary has not changed in over 20 years, and it probably never will—as long as there are fresh-faced foreigners deplaning at Narita Airport in search of their fortunes. Don't take a fulltime position unless the salary warrants giving up that much of your time. I promise you, if you consider all the jobs I describe in *FIT*, you can make *at least* ¥250,000 a month just freelancing part-time *and* have your freedom to pursue whatever other dreams you have while you are here.

- There seems to be a philosophy in Japan that employees should not necessarily be paid overtime. As a freelancer you shouldn't encounter this situation. If you do, communicate with your superior and negotiate your overtime pay. Don't be aggressive; just address it politely and firmly. If you become involved socially or romantically with a Japanese person who must work overtime, he/she may argue that it's *shoganai* (meaning "nothing can be done" about a situation). Not true. They can go through the same channels anyone does when they are unhappy with their workload. The difference is the fear factor instilled in them by a group mentality. Do not subscribe to this mentality for one minute. I have seen many foreigners who think they must "be Japanese" in order to succeed here. You can respect, appreciate and learn from your Japanese colleagues; it does not mean you must also accept whatever situation you are presented with.

- When you become too busy to negotiate everything on your own in Japanese, hiring a bilingual Japanese person on occasion can make life much easier. (Note: If you are already working for a company with bilingual employees, do not be afraid to ask one for help. But do *not* take advantage of them or look to them to solve all your language-related issues in Japan—unless you plan to offer them compensation.)

- *You have hidden skills!* You may not realize that the dance class you joined for fun, the public speaking course you took at community college or the business letters you composed for your boss have any particular value, but you will discover you can apply most of your life experiences in a positive, income-producing way in Japan.

- The most important thing to know about working in Japan is: *Japan pays you to learn.* Meaning: while you may not have the requisite skills for a particular job, if the Japanese perceive you as a kind, honest person and/or you have some other desirable "foreign" quality (which can't always be determined, but sometimes includes blonde hair/blue eyes, R&B singing skills or an appearance similar to a short list of beloved celebrities, including the late actress Audrey Hepburn), you may be given opportunities you never dreamed of (and some not worth dreaming of). As a result, you get paid to learn; remember that and you will prosper here.

- The list of freelance jobs in *FIT* is not all-inclusive, but the beauty of freelancing in Tokyo is that if you do any of the jobs in this chapter, they will lead to others. Remember that, too, and you will prosper here. Note: Further research about freelance jobs can be done on the *FIT* site (§ "Employment Opportunities").

When To Look for Work

Japan operates on a fiscal year from April 1 to March 31. This means most jobs are available from April 1 (and are often not advertised until exactly April 1). While freelance work is available year-round, April 1 still marks the beginning of the "new year" when the cherry blossoms appear, the weather warms up and people are generally in a good mood. As such the job pickings are more plentiful and it's the best time to secure a position or establish a relationship with the type of company or individual you would like to work for. For those who have not yet moved here, do your best to get set up by mid-February or so, certainly no later than March, and start networking. You *will* find work.

Another great time for freelancers is during the jungle-hot summer season. Those lucky (or dumb?) enough to take a holiday leave behind a smattering of good voice and acting jobs, so those of you who have stayed behind can clean up—if you can stand the heat.

Okay, we've got a few basics out of the way. You are ready to start work and make lots of money. Good, because, as I mentioned in "Why Freelance in Tokyo?", there is no reason you can't earn between US$50-75K annually if you are willing to occasionally burn the midnight oil and learn how to creatively schedule your freelance jobs.

ENGLISH LANGUAGE-RELATED JOBS

TEACHING ENGLISH

Teacher: You can't meet your friend "on" the airport.

Student: Why not?

In Japan, studying English is part of the curriculum for junior and senior high school students, meaning most Japanese have studied English for six years before they enter the work force. Despite this, many of them still have trouble speaking it. This is not a comment on their ability to learn English. English is not easy to learn nor is it essential for the Japanese to speak it. (Remember that when you come marching into Tokyo expecting everyone to understand what you're saying.)

However, Japan recognizes its place in the international community and since English continues to be the *lingua franca* for the Internet and many international businesses, lucrative opportunities still exist for native English speakers able to teach ESL (English as a Second Language) classes at language schools, public schools and major corporations.

That said, despite what you can earn as an English teacher in Tokyo (see "Salary" below), it is my strong, strong, **strong** opinion ***not*** to pursue this line of work—unless you really *are* an English teacher with a degree in English or TEFL (Teaching English as a Foreign Language) or otherwise have a *deep* desire to teach English to Japanese people. If this is not you, and you *still* want to pursue this line of work, make sure (by taking advantage of the jobs listed in this chapter) that teaching English is only *a launching pad* to help you get started on a successful career as a freelancer in Tokyo.

Present, Future, Pluperfect: How I Became an English Teacher in Tokyo

As I had come to Japan to pursue a music business career, teaching English never crossed my mind. Until I found my dream job, I took a gig playing piano in Ginza (Tokyo's Beverly Hills) six nights a week. One day an American woman I had met called to say she was leaving Japan and asked me to finish the last two months of her teaching contract at a Japanese chemical company. At first I said no; when she said the monthly salary was ¥250,000 for 20 hours a week (Mon-Fri, 1:00pm-5:00pm), I decided to do it, as it would still give me mornings to pursue my job search.

At the interview I offered my English language résumé, which contained *nothing* to indicate my suitability as an English teacher. My only other competition was a younger man who, I was told later, was not appropriately dressed. I got the job. Lesson: Press that suit and be ready to wear it!

My only training took place during my acquaintance's last two days on the job. Fortunately she had teaching skills; I imitated her upbeat style until I got my own rhythm. I finished the contract and, to my amazement, was asked to stay for an additional six months. When I made it clear I was a musician, not an English teacher, I was told: "Sometimes *personality* outweighs *experience*." On that basis I agreed to stay. Lesson: Be cheerful!

While I would never say that teaching English in Tokyo was my calling in life, it gave me great insight into corporate Japan and *paid me to learn* how to do something that helped me earn a tremendous amount of money in the years to come.

Salary

While in the past English teachers were hired directly by a school or company, at present most teachers are hired through screening agencies to make sure no unqualified weirdos get through (that doesn't mean the screening process is successful). This has value for the school/company, but not for you—you will most likely receive a lower salary from the agencies than if you were to get clients on your own.

Agencies generally offer hourly rates of ¥2,000-4,000, rarely more. Places that hire English-language teachers directly pay hourly rates as low as ¥1,000—but as high as ¥5,000 or more. The rates vary depending on a long list of factors including where you'll teach (schools, conversation cafés, companies), who you'll teach (i.e. company presidents) and the type of English you'll teach (daily conversation, business, preparation for TOEIC [the Test of English for International Communication]), etc.

Having a Masters Degree (in anything) *may* get you more, but not necessarily. Also: If you go through an agency, you will most likely be expected to provide *copious* notes (written during your free time) on each student's progress, as well as exactly what you have taught in each lesson. Also, if you have to cancel for illness, etc., you must provide the agency with a lesson plan for that class. This adds up to endless hours of paperwork.

You will also see advertised the ubiquitous monthly salary of anywhere between ¥200,000-250,000. This is not only the standard salary for teaching English; it is considered enough to survive on. Correct: It's enough to survive on—and that's all. For this amount of money, expect to work 20-25 hours or more (sometimes a lot more) a week. The clincher: Some companies expect you to sign an iron-clad contract that requires you to be available for a certain number of hours each day (anywhere between 8:00 a.m. and 8:00 p.m.) while the company "coordinates" the schedules of its students. In other words, while you may only work "20-25 hours" a week, you have to be available for 60 hours a week! This is slave labor; you can't plan your day until the last minute. Don't waste time with these companies! Before joining any *eikaiwa* (English-language conversation) school, ask questions up front, check out Internet message boards, and do not, under any circumstances, allow this type of company to be your visa sponsor or sign *any* agreement indenturing you to them for any length of time.

If you decide to pursue this line of work, your job is to avoid the glut of agencies acting as middlemen between clients and teachers and *secure your own private students* and/or company classes (see this chapter, "Helpful Hints"). Again, why is this important? You will discover by reading *FIT* that it is possible to land high-paying freelance jobs as an actor (TV commercials), model (print ads) and voice actor (TV commercials, corporate videos, English-language study guides, etc.) in Tokyo. In order to obtain these types of jobs you must have a *flexible schedule.* If you sign a contract with an agency to teach English for any kind of company, your schedule will be very difficult, if not impossible, to adjust. Calling in sick is really not an option.

As for company classes, you can earn between ¥5,000-7,000 an hour or more. If you're lucky enough to connect with politicians or celebrities, you can sometimes command as high as ¥10,000 an hour.

By teaching privately you set a schedule convenient for *you,* teach whom you are comfortable teaching, control the amount of paperwork you do (if any), take holidays when you please and work when you want. It's all possible.

But... there are even more reasons why you should only teach privately. Here is a true-to-life scenario: Jobless, you go to great trouble to secure a part-time position with Happy English Learning, Ltd. or HELL, for short.

HELL will farm you out to the Denshi Electric Company, located somewhere in an isolated village that requires two trains and a bus to reach, on Tuesdays and Thursdays from 6-7:30 p.m. at the "generous" evening rate of ¥4,000 per hour for a ten-week period. After tax you receive ¥5,400 for 90 minutes of work (plus transportation fees). You are *not* paid for the 90 minutes of travel time or the 30 minutes to prepare a lesson plan, grade papers, or fill out some form explaining why Mr. Yamada is failing. In reality you are putting in four hours for ¥5,400. You'll get ¥10,800 for twice weekly lessons for a period of 10 weeks, with a grand total of ¥108,000 for 60 hours or ¥1,800 per hour.

Other than shattering your vision of becoming a millionaire by teaching English, why is this important? Because, with a little effort on your part, you might score a TV commercial that pays between ¥100,000-400,000 for approximately one day's work. However, be aware: Even after everything has been scheduled and agreed upon, entire productions can be canceled at a moment's notice. So, while you may have gone to the trouble of securing a substitute to cover your contracted English lesson, you will now not only *not* have a TV commercial, you'll also be out ¥5,400—which could have bought a nice bag of apples. Regardless, being *available* for that *possible* high-paying TV commercial is one of the reasons why you might actually get it.

What to do? Form a small company (nothing legally binding) between you and at least two other trusted native English-speaking friends who could teach one another's (private or privately-obtained) classes at a moment's notice. This type of "company" may also lead to offers of other types of jobs (proofreading, editing, writing) that require a native English speaker. In other words: find a small group of people you can trust, cover as much territory as you can and share the wealth.

What You Need to Know

Experience not required—or is it?

Do you need experience to teach English in Japan? No. Should you have experience? Yes. You should have legitimate teaching experience and/or a certificate in teaching ESL. Without one or the other you risk the following: If you think you can teach English, I dare you to do it right now: Give a lesson to a friend/relative and see if they understand what you are teaching. As you teach, focus on how you feel, listen to your voice, be aware of your body language. Are you sitting in a chair, staring at a book, telling people to repeat things? Are you moving about, tossing out questions, challenging and invigorating people? Can you explain the finer points of the English language at the drop of a hat? Do you have a clue in hell what you are talking about? Think about these things, please.

If you are still gung-ho on doing this, let me tell you what I learned as a "non-teacher teacher:" *Be prepared.* This means have a *lesson plan*—or risk rambling for 90 minutes by reaching out to the universe for word games or memories from high school English classes, or making desperate attempts to connect to students via sports, movie stars and/or endless Qs&As about students' lives. You will feel like an ass—and look like one, too. Some people might say you can wing it; I say you can wing it only after you've gotten the hang of it—and that might take a long time. So, again, you can "teach" English in Japan... but whether or not students are being "taught" is a matter of opinion.

I Can Do It!

You still may be thinking: "I can do it. What's the big deal?" There isn't one—if you're a legitimate teacher familiar with lesson plans, progress reports, grading and comment cards. If you aren't, picture yourself having to (sometimes) teach English from books containing dated conversations, attempting to engage students (some whom might be sleeping, texting or putting sparkly flowers on their nails) in those conversations. Are you *in* the picture—or headed back to Narita airport?

If you respond to any ad for an English teaching job (all which offer similar salaries), be prepared if called for an interview to teach a sample lesson. In this lesson you will be expected to quickly engage your "student" in a conversation. This "student," a Japanese person, who may be a company employee or a real language student, may or may not have English-speaking ability. After you've done this type of sample lesson often enough you will find yourself using the word "hobby" (as in "What is your hobby?"). The Japanese know this English word and understandably like to use English words they know. So, while it might be okay to "hobby" your way into your first teaching job, let me ask: Would you use the word "hobby" in daily conversation unless you're somebody's nut uncle who collects stamps and lives in a one-room apartment facing a brick wall?

Market Yourself

Avoid situations mentioned above by marketing yourself. One way that you can do this might surprise you: Post simple ads with your phone number, e-mail address and professional photo on the community bulletin boards found throughout suburban areas (but start near your place of residence). They might be torn down by community do-gooders who feel you don't have the right to post them without authorization from some "higher authority" (read "them"), but post anyway. The Japanese who contact you are those who *want* to communicate with a foreigner. Remember, that's *you*.

In addition to posting ads on community bulletin boards, registering with job websites and exchanging *meishi*, do research. Don't be afraid to cold-call companies you'd like to work for (larger companies almost always have an English speaker available to assist you). Tell them you have an interest in working for them as a teacher, editor, proofreader, etc. In the event there is no English speaker available, I have provided you with an opening dialogue in Japanese to get you started ("Telephone/Work-related phrases").

If the company expresses interest, provide them with your website or online profile/résumé (sometimes referred to as "CV"), always ensuring you feature a face photo. Some companies may reject you because they will ultimately decide to go with a hiring agency; others may be interested because you took it upon yourself to contact them directly. (Note: Salaries offered at some of these companies *may not* necessarily vary greatly from what the agencies are offering, but you *will* have more control over your schedule *and* choice of teaching materials if you get the job on your own.)

If a company wants to hire you directly, it most likely will expect you to sign a contract. This means: since you would have no agency to turn to, problems could arise if you ever needed to bring in a substitute teacher (editor, etc.). However, if you stay with the company long enough, you should be able to introduce a qualified individual to occasionally take over your class(es) if you happen to land a high-paying TV commercial or voice job (see this chapter, "Actors/Extras/Models" and "Voice Actors").

What the Japanese Want From You

Unless you are helping a Japanese person prepare for the TOEIC or coaching them how to handle foreign business matters in Japan or abroad, when the Japanese take English lessons they are hoping for a pleasant experience with a nice, kind foreigner, preferably young and attractive, and, most importantly, someone who hasn't been in Japan too long. If you are already savvy about Japan, it might work against you. Advice: Play dumb. The Japanese love to go on about their food and their way of life and are keen to know if you've "adjusted." This provides grist for thousands of lessons. So: if you appear to have a sincere interest in Japan, its people and its food, not only should you be able to teach enough lessons to give you all the pocket money you could ever want, you should gain a cultural sensitivity to Japan, as well.

Get the Students You Want

Be specific in your ads about whom you are willing to teach:

- Age: children, teens, college students, adults
- Level: beginners, intermediate, advanced
- Type: students, office workers, seniors, LGBT

I specifically mention seniors and LGBT as I feel they are overlooked in Japanese society—and you could carve out a niche in the marketplace by catering to them. Many seniors worked hard on their English when they were younger and never got a chance to use it. Personally, I found they were the most enthusiastic students. As for LGBT students, many hope to find someone understanding and accepting of their situation.

Meishi/Website

Do not limit yourself to just being an "English teacher." Increase your chances for other jobs by listing, for example, the following on your *meishi* (in English, followed by Japanese):

Writer • English Teacher • Editor • Narrator*
作家•英語の教師 • 編集者 • ナレーター

*In Japan, voice actors are often referred to as narrators. See this chapter, "Voice Actor."

On the back of the *meishi* briefly list (in Japanese) your credits, honors, degrees, etc. I have found this type of *meishi* (as opposed to the standard *meishi* with the exact same information in English on one side/Japanese on the other) is the charm—*especially* if it has your professional-looking photo on the front.

Your website/online profile should state (as your ad did) the levels/students you teach, class size, rates, etc. Some people don't like to post rates, but by doing so, you will attract the type of student who is willing to pay for *you*. Remember: Sell *yourself*; aim *high*.

Fees/Incentives/Cancellations

- Set a fair price of ¥10,000 for a group of 3-4 students or ¥7,000 for 1-2 students for a 90-minute lesson.

- Try not to teach an hour lesson for less than ¥4,000-5,000. If you drop it to less than ¥4,000 you will be like every other hungry teacher in town. Ask for the higher fee and you will attract the type of student that thinks you have more to offer—which, of course, you do!

- Offer incentives by giving a free or discounted lesson after every 10 lessons. Do this by giving the student a *pointo kādo* (point card), a *meishi*-sized card filled with squares you stamp or initial after a student takes a lesson. The Japanese love point cards. They are offered everywhere, from drugstores to department stores. Make your own and reap the benefits: repeat customers.

- Do not entrap students by saying they must take a certain number of lessons. Be as flexible with them as you will want them to be with you.

- Have a cancellation policy. Suggestion: You or your student should be allowed to cancel 24 hours before the scheduled lesson. This is important for those odd times when you receive a TV commercial or voice job that may pay ¥100,000-300,000 for a day's work. If you or the student cancel the same day, you must offer a free lesson or they must pay the full lesson price.

Teaching Materials/What to Wear/What and Where to Teach

- First and foremost, find out what the student wants to learn—and focus on that. By teaching the student what he/she wants to learn, the lesson becomes a rewarding experience for both of you. If it's anything else, stop doing it or get advice from the hundreds of other language teachers you will meet in Tokyo and redefine your approach.

- Always dress professionally. That means business attire, not t-shirts and jeans.

- Always carry your *meishi* with you and give one to your student. This shows you are serious and will help you network and discover other jobs.

- Teach at Starbucks (or, as the Japanese say, *sutāba*). It is not necessary to order anything. Just get a glass of water and sit at a table. Your student also may not order anything—although he/she may offer to buy you a coffee. (Do not expect it.) One way or the other, there aren't "Table Police" checking to see who has or hasn't ordered, so, voilà: instant classroom at your service.

- Do not teach at your apartment or the student's apartment unless conditions are ideal. The reasons are clear: If you or your student is hoping to find a sex partner or spouse, "private lessons" certainly offer unique opportunities. But if you are here to earn money as a teacher and hope to get recommendations from your students, give careful thought as to where you hold your lessons.

- Check with your local *kuyakusho* (ward / town office) or *shiyakusho* (city hall) (see § "Ward Offices"). The *kuyakusho* and *shiyakusho* are akin to community centers. They offer perks to the citizens of their towns, such as public meeting rooms (small, medium, large). You must reserve them (sometimes months in advance), but the fee is incredibly reasonable and the rooms (at least in my ward) are clean and bright. You must explain to the staff what you will be using the room for (i.e. an English conversation class, writing class, etc), but keep in mind you are not supposed to "conduct business" in these rooms. Payment for lessons must be discreet; that's the best advice I can give. (Note: It's unlikely you will find English-speaking staff at these facilities, but there may be a specific day / time when an English speaker is available and a notice indicating such should be posted.)

- Decide what you think you can teach (i.e. business, general conversation, grammar), and either purchase an online textbook or buy a hard copy that provides *very short* lessons and simple worksheets (for your students) that can be copied or downloaded from the Internet.

- Do not immediately force the student to buy the (online or hard copy) textbook you want to use. For the first few lessons bring copies of the material you plan to cover. If the student is happy and decides to continue with you, suggest he / she buy the textbook.

- Reinforcing the lesson by playing recorded phrases is helpful but difficult to do in a coffeehouse, so having your own teaching space is preferable. If you need to model a two-part conversation until the student feels comfortable enough to participate, a simple way to do so is to raise your right hand for "voice A," your left for "voice B." This approach has worked well for me.

What You Can Expect

If you choose to work for a company or school, below are examples of classes you might be asked to teach. As for textbooks, they have sometimes been chosen by the company, an agency or a previous teacher. You may also be asked to recommend something (which you will be able to do once you visit Kinokuniya bookstore in Tokyo and research their extensive ESL section; see § "Tips for Teaching English").

(Note: Some companies/schools use staff to monitor your classes; don't be surprised if someone suddenly shows up to observe you. Also, some companies/schools put you on a three-month probation to make sure you know what you're doing.)

- Company lessons: Classes with 2-10 students, usually twice a week for a period of 90 minutes, usually in the morning or evening, before or after the work day.

- Full- or part-time positions at junior high, high schools or vocational schools: Classes with 10-30 students and anywhere between 20-25 hours of teaching time (but the endless hours of prep, filling out forms, grading homework and other paper/life-wasting activities are *not* paid for).

- Intensives: One-day to one-week classes with 2-20 students (usually company employees) to help prepare them for a specific situation which will require them to use English.

- Teaching at chain English schools: Classes of 1-6 students, with lessons that last upwards from 40 minutes.

- Private lessons: Requested by companies where you are already employed or by individuals you meet through networking. Lesson times are up to you and the student, but shouldn't be shorter than an hour or longer than 90 minutes.

- Online/telephone lessons: Depending on the company you work for, teaching online/telephone lessons may allow you to work from home at a time that's convenient for you as well as the student.

Helpful Hints

- By establishing relationships with a few excellent private students (including corporate clients), you can teach when it suits you and easily add between ¥100,000-200,000 a month to your bank account, leaving you with the time and energy to do other things with your life.

- While you may be thinking of how much money you can get, *some of the people taking classes from you actually want to learn something*! Be clear: If you decide to teach English in Tokyo, think of each student as someone you love *dearly,* and treat them accordingly. There is nothing worse than the righteous attitude that some Westerners have displayed here when they fake their way through teaching English and then don't understand why their students don't "respond." Yes, some students study English only because their companies require them to. Regardless, you need to be there for that one person who wants to learn (and there *will* be one); after all, you are an English teacher… aren't you?

- Instead of just thinking about teaching English conversation, consider teaching business English writing classes. If you can really explain how to write a bona fide business letter, you will not only be doing the business world a great service, but, as you won't have to talk as much, there will be much less wear-and-tear on your throat. (Note: If the company where you teach does not offer this kind of class, suggest they consider adding it.)

- Let every English-language teacher you meet know that you will substitute for them. This does *not* mean steal their students or hard-earned jobs! You might be asked (by the company employing them) to replace them, but *don't do it*. If you want to talk about bad karma, this is it.

- Avoid teaching for chain schools. One tragedy that befell English teachers in Japan was when its largest English-language chain school, NOVA, went bankrupt — leaving the teachers without pay and/or a visa sponsor. Not only do chain schools pay what amounts to minimum wage, you are "chained" to them in ways you can't imagine and will never have the freedom to pursue the great opportunities available to you as an English-speaking foreigner in Tokyo.

- Keep a list of all English textbooks you use. Why? When you show up for an interview to teach "business English" at a big corporation, they may ask you what textbooks you are familiar with. Knowledge of current/popular textbooks might be the deciding factor when a company is determining which individual to hire. As mentioned, if you are not familiar with English language textbooks, a visit to the ESL section at Kinokuniya bookstore is in order (§ "Tips for Teaching English"). Thumb through textbooks that appeal to you; make a note of them. They all basically follow the same format, the differences being some are laid out better than others and some have teacher's manuals (*extremely* helpful if you are not a professional English teacher).

- Never refer to yourself as *eigo no sensei* (lit. "master of English"); instead say *Watashi wa eigo no kyōshi desu* ("I am a teacher of English) or (*Watashi wa*) *eigo no kyōshi o shite imasu* (roughly, "I do [the job of] teaching English"). *Kyōshi* is a general title for classroom teachers.

- While it is *not* necessary to have any Japanese vocabulary to teach English in Japan, knowing a few key words to explain grammar can be helpful. To that end, see "Tips for Teaching English" on the *FIT* website under Helpful Websites.

- Remember: You are special! By offering short-term, fun, private lessons, you provide a unique opportunity for the Japanese to interact with a nice, professional Westerner. You also offer an alternative to students who otherwise might shell out lots of money to participate in never-ending programs at English-language chain schools.

ENGLISH LANGUAGE-RELATED JOBS

TEACHING YOUR SPECIALTY

Teach housewives how to cook coq au vin? Uh… sure!

If you have special skills (cooking, dancing, singing, playing an instrument, acting, etc.), you can definitely teach them in Tokyo. (See this chapter, "Entrepreneurial Endeavors" if you want to take things a step further.) Again: *You are special.* You are a stranger in a strange land, speaking a strange language. Take advantage of your strangeness! The reality is that the Japanese are willing, if you present yourself in a winning, cheerful way, to take a chance and learn something from you, the Exotic Foreigner. Yes, even in this day and age, whatever you bring to the table, so to speak, might be tempting enough for Japanese people to want to learn more about. (Note: Other English-speaking foreigners may also want to join your class. See this chapter, "What You Can Expect.")

Here is a short list of lessons you might consider teaching:

- Acting (diction, dialects, improvisation, scene work)
- Aerobics
- Anything to do with make-up, hair or nails
- Ballroom dancing
- Creative writing (short stories, screenwriting)
- Ethnic cooking
- Massage
- Piano (classical, pop, jazz)
- Singing (opera, Broadway, R&B… you name it)
- Songwriting
- Tap dancing
- Website design
- Yoga

"French Chef" for a Day!

My "specialties" included teaching piano and voice. I soon found the odd student who was happy to take music lessons from the new foreigner in town; little did I know I was also a French chef! It all began the day a Canadian woman I knew called and said, "You like to cook, don't you?" I said yes; next thing, I was being interviewed to teach a half-day cooking class (in English), offered by the Tokyo Gas Company (basically to help sell the gas appliances used to prepare the meal for the class). The fact I had only cooked my own meals for two or three people in my tiny *manshon* didn't matter; the main requirement for the class was that a native English speaker teach it.

At the interview I was nervous, becoming more so as I realized the interviewer really could not speak English. As for the menu I would be teaching, I had brought several sample recipes with me, not paying any special attention to them. But once the interviewer saw a *coq au vin* recipe, she suddenly decided I would prepare a French feast!

I practiced my "feast" twice, in my mini-kitchen, talking aloud as I "became" a French chef. One week later, shaved, showered and be-aproned, I stood before 20 smiling Japanese housewives in a room which could only be described as the set of a fantastic cooking show. I even had an assistant to hand me any utensil I might need to "create" my masterpiece! The only things missing were a TV camera and a studio audience.

Somehow over the next four hours, I and my students managed to whip up something edible. Everyone was happy with the final result, and I left ¥30,000 richer and a much better cook than I had been. In fact, I went on to become an excellent cook and often ended up preparing holiday dinners for homesick *gaijin* stuck in Tokyo during the Christmas season. Lesson: As mentioned, and clearly confirmed here, Japan pays you to learn.

Salary

Because you are teaching a specialty, charge more. It's my opinion the average rate for any specialty should be a minimum of ¥7,000 per hour, certainly not less than ¥5,000. If you ask for less, you end up doing an English lesson. Test the waters: ¥10,000 per hour may not be unreasonable if you really have the skills you say you do.

Even if you ultimately find that what you can get paid to teach a "specialty" class is not necessarily higher than what you'd earn to teach English, you can at least teach something you enjoy that does not require you to differentiate past, present and future perfect tenses. (And now I can finally ask what's haunted me since seventh grade: Since we don't know what the future holds, how could it possibly be perfect?)

What You Need to Know

As mentioned in "Teaching English," have a résumé, advertisement or website prepared—always with a photo of you and your great smile—that clearly states what you do (in E-J for best results). No one is likely to question your ability, but having a degree, certificate or legitimate credits will certainly help.

What You Can Expect

The Japanese students who attend these types of classes are looking to enjoy a cultural experience, one that doesn't require opening an English grammar book. There may also be other students from other parts of the world who do not speak English fluently, as well as native English-speaking students.

So, make this a "win-win" situation: Teach what you love and they will love what you teach. While you may not have as many students as you would if you were simply teaching English conversation, you can still create a situation pleasurable for all.

Helpful Hints

- Where to teach: If you don't have enough space at home to teach these courses, you can (for all but cooking, obviously) rent a dance/rehearsal studio, or, as mentioned in "Teaching English," reserve a meeting room at your *kuyakusho*. If you teach English for a company, ask if there's a room they aren't using after hours or on weekends. If so, offer to rent it for a small fee; voilà—you have a space of your own.

- Point cards: Use the "point card" system mentioned earlier. Give a free/discounted lesson after every 10 or so. This encourages "repeat customers" and the Japanese think it's *kawaii* (cute). If they actually take that many lessons from you, you'll be happy to give them the free/discounted lesson.

- Acting: There is no reason you can't teach acting in Japan. You have a great opportunity to teach diction, movement, etc. If you are good, you will be of great value to those Japanese who dream of getting a chance to be in a legitimate Hollywood/European movie, and who will be grateful some wonderful teacher (you) helped them.

- Aerobics/Yoga: Do not be afraid to approach any fitness club (see § "Fitness Clubs") and tell them you are interested in teaching for them. Yoga can be taught anywhere you can rent a dance studio. For either exercise, though, unless you are bilingual or have your routines worked out so you can do them in Japanese, finding this kind of work may be challenging.

- Cooking: Have a special ethnic dish you can prepare? Know some unusual recipes you can pull out of your chef's hat at a moment's notice? This knowledge can all be put to use in Tokyo. On occasion, you will see ads requesting foreigners to teach cooking classes in English. Generally speaking, these pay more than standard English classes for approximately two-to-three hours of your time. Why shouldn't you be the teacher?

- Voice/Instruments: If you teach voice or piano/guitar, etc., you can just as easily post the same types of ads mentioned earlier or make the appropriate website. (Note: You might find classified ads requesting a qualified music teacher to teach in English. However, these classes only pay between ¥4,000-5,000 an hour, and just because the students may think they want to learn about music from a native English-speaking teacher doesn't mean that they can speak English.)

ENGLISH LANGUAGE-RELATED JOBS

COPYEDITOR / COPYWRITER / EDITOR PROOFREADER / REWRITER

"Let's aim to deepen our mutual understanding with heartful feelings!"

These jobs are technically different, but many companies in Tokyo require someone who can do them all. Be prepared.

Tall Buildings: How I Became a Copywriter in Tokyo

Though I had always been an "A" English student, I never pictured myself doing any writing other than songwriting. But as a native English speaker in Tokyo, I was, almost from the day I arrived, given translated J-E documents to proofread or rewrite. Although I had no professional experience, I suddenly found myself working as a proofreader/rewriter for a company that translated a wide variety of documents, from business letters to contracts. I didn't really know what I was doing; again, I was paid to learn.

While some documents were translated by people so gifted I was embarrassed to check their work, others... well, let's say I learned English was more "flexible" than I thought it could be. Example: All documents seemed to contain a reference to nature—regardless of what the document's subject was. Everything had to be "green" or "lush"—even if the point of reference was a stone cold cement building. Other documents included unique uses of English verbs, such as one that described a mother "milking" a baby. When I suggested to the translator that perhaps she meant "nursing" a baby, she put up a vociferous fight as to why her phrase was correct. I attempted to reason with her, but soon realized she wasn't going to let go of her beloved "verb." After years of this work, I came to accept these challenges as a way to broaden my linguistic abilities.

Salary

Unless you have bilingual knowledge of technical terms connected with the automotive, financial, legal or medical fields, the salaries for the jobs mentioned in this section are not substantially different those for English teachers.

Rates range from ¥2,000-5,000 an hour, depending on the difficulty of the subject matter. If you're working by the page, you can earn as much as ¥1,000 for proofing a page, or ¥1,000-1,500 for editing/rewriting a page, again depending on the difficulty of the subject matter.

What You Need to Know

Do you know your proofreader marks? (§ "Proofreader Marks") Can you turn a poorly translated document into a polished gem of writing? Are you prepared to repeatedly encounter (and accept) questionable uses of English as well as set-in-stone words/phrases the Japanese seem intent on using in many of their translated documents? Can you accept the beautifully rewritten phrases you've sweated to come up with being returned to their original badly-worded messes because "that's what the client wants"?

If yes to all of the above, you can find this type of work by answering ads or going through agencies... but why bother? Find your own assignments: As you've been doing, continue to hand out your *meishi*, post your ads, set up a website, cold-call companies you think might use your talents ("Telephone"), and/or send letters to them with samples of your work. To strengthen your position, consider partnering with a qualified freelance J-E translator/interpreter. The two of you can make a powerful team, and, if truly motivated, can get some choice assignments that may lead to bigger and better projects.

The advantage of doing writing work in this day and age is that many assignments can be done via e-mail. Even so, if possible, first visit a potential client by dropping by their office. Face-to-face time still counts in Japan, so make your professional presence known.

When you interview for writing positions, you may be prompted to indicate your field of expertise. If not, you may be expected to handle documents covering any of the following:

- Automotive
- Banking/Finance
- Company Brochures
- Contracts
- Corporate reports
- Cosmetic products

- Legal (usually simple agreements/contracts)*
- Medical/Pharmaceutical)
- Speeches
- Website content

It may be assumed you can proof any document related to the above topics because you're a native English speaker. Having been in this situation, do what I did: learn the necessary vocabulary as quickly as possible and upgrade your skill level.

(*Note: It is not the duty of the proofreader to determine whether legal documents are, in fact, legal. But, regrettably, legal "interpretations" may be encountered. If this is the case, consider pointing them out to your superior. Otherwise, let it go; they are not paying you to be a lawyer.)

What You Can Expect

You are usually given documents that have been translated at breakneck speed and which you are expected to refashion into breathtaking prose (also at breakneck speed).

If you are working directly at an employer's/client's office, you may find yourself twiddling your thumbs for the majority of the day until some harried individual materializes at your desk at 4:45 p.m. with an assignment that "must be done instantly." This is the type of job you want, as you will be able to use the rest of the day doing writing/proofreading work for other companies. I did this for years and no one ever once commented on it.

While working at a client's office, you may also be asked to transcribe speeches, news reports or televised interviews. (See this chapter, "Transcriber.") This is an unpleasant task, but expect you will be asked to do it.

Regardless of the writing "hat" you are wearing at any given moment, an employer may also casually ask you to create slogans that should be handled by advertising agencies. If you are presented with this task, I suggest you politely refuse—even at the risk of losing your job. People who work at advertising agencies are generally paid a great deal of money to write catchy phrases to sell products. If the company you work for wants to negotiate a separate amount for this task, great; if not, think carefully about doing it, or you might see the wonderful words you wrote for ¥3,500 an hour plastered across a huge billboard for a product that has a multi-million yen advertising campaign.

Helpful Hints

Many Japanese are, as anyone who has learned another language would be, proud of their ability to speak, read and write English; frankly, they should be. Except for an increasing amount of *gairaigo* (foreign "loan" words, often English), there is *no* connection between English and Japanese. When you hear a Japanese speaking English, trust that he/she has put in a lot of time and effort to be able to do so.

However, along with that pride sometimes comes a certain stubbornness or fear. With translations, some translators will insist on certain "set" words and phrases. You will frequently encounter such set-in-stone expressions as: "Their aim is to deepen international friendship and mutual understanding between the two cultures." At first you'll think, "Okay, whatever, great." But when you see this same expression 50 times a day, you will want to become an arsonist, torching the very document you're holding. To overcome this desire, first suggest the translator use something different. Better yet, take the time and make a phrase list for your company of natural phrases as opposed to stock translations. I did this, but even then, people were receptive to them only 50% of the time (but better than not at all).

Another annoying thing is that when you use the Internet to research or confirm a word/phrase that sounds unusual to you, you will often find it—on a Japanese site with a translated English page. All of the sudden, the questionable word/phrase is now "legitimate"—and yet, it still doesn't make any sense. Please do not use these words/phrases, no matter what your client or employer says. Tell them (politely) unless the word/phrase is also used on native English-language sites, just because someone in Japan thought it sounded good doesn't mean it does. You will be told, "The Japanese understand what this means." Acknowledge their comment politely, but be firm and say, "It doesn't have any meaning and will not be understood by native English speakers."

Alternatively, *do not assume* the translated word/phrase you are reading is incorrect. I have eaten humble pie many a time because I was foolish enough to believe I couldn't possibly be wrong.

Note: Doing this type of work will help you become familiar with industry-specific Japanese words/phrases that you most likely would not learn otherwise. Be smart: Make a list of them and keep them handy. If your company downsizes and your job evaporates, you can confidently move to a new position because you've taken the time to learn those words/phrases that few native English speakers ever will.

Also, these types of writing jobs can only make you a better writer. I strongly suggest if you turn out a fine piece of prose from a ghastly grammatical mess, keep it—and the mess. Have five of these from different fields and include them in your portfolio. Remove any sensitive information (proper names, brand names, addresses, etc.) and post these examples on your website. While companies interested in your skills will still most likely ask you to do a "trial" rewrite of some questionable translation, suggest they *first* look at your pretty pieces of prose—they may come in handy if you ever need to produce a quick sample of your writing ability.

❖

ENGLISH LANGUAGE-RELATED JOBS

FREELANCE WRITER

"For the last three months, I have been inexplicably drawn to tea shops with pastel color schemes."

There are a limited number of English-language newspapers and magazines (or their web equivalents) that cater to Tokyo's native English-speaking community, as well as to Japanese people with varying degrees of English fluency. Once you start reading these publications, it will occur to you that you can write articles as good as the ones you're reading; I encourage you to do so. This is a field often overlooked because it is assumed someone has to be a professional in order to get published. Not true. It *is* true that if you can't bring your game to the table, the likelihood of getting published on a frequent basis may not occur, but don't let that stop you.

Have Pen, Will Travel: How I Became a Pro Writer

After living in Tokyo a few years I realized I was spending a fair amount of time in coffee shops between freelance assignments. I imagined there were many others like myself and decided to put my coffee shop time to good use. I sent a query letter to an editor at *The Japan Times* suggesting a column about interesting coffee shops in Tokyo. It didn't surprise me when the editor did not respond; I had no journalistic background and no sample articles to show my ability.

Two years later, still desiring to write a column (and still without writing samples), I sent the exact same letter (save for the date) to the same editor at *The Japan Times*; this time I followed up with a phone call. The editor, a Japanese woman, took my call as if she had been waiting for it. "Yes," she said, "we would like to run that column." Within a week I had my first article published about unique *kissaten* (coffee/tea shops) in the Tokyo area, followed by a monthly column that ran for two years. Again, I got paid to learn.

My column led to other assignments for English-language newspapers and magazines, and ultimately this book. So, for someone who did not have a journalistic background, I feel I've done just fine, thanks to my freelance writing opportunities in Tokyo.

Salary

Articles pay from ¥5,000-40,000. What you earn is based on any/all of the following: word count (anywhere between 500-2000 words), type of article (feature, essay, review) and type of publication (newspaper, magazine, website). Also, if you have taken photos for your articles, you *may* receive up to ¥5,000 for each photo used.

The above fees, like those for other jobs in this book, have not changed in years nor are they likely to soon. Essentially, whether you are a novice or seasoned pro, expect to be paid the same.

What You Need to Know

Have an idea for a column or an article? Know someone famous or semi-famous you can profile? Visited some out-of-the-way place and have a write-up for it? Great. Call or send query letters to any of the § listed on the *FIT* website under "Media."

From the local papers and magazines you won't get rich, but you can get your name in print, get paid and add a feather to your cap. Some catty people, though, will not acknowledge anything you've written in Japan as being "real" journalism. Screw them; you're here to make money and get experience.

On the other hand, if you're a novice, have an editor friend read your "masterpiece" before you submit it. There are plenty of great writers in Tokyo vying for the same limited number of spots in the local English-language media. Don't let that intimidate you—but don't live in a fantasy world, either. While I had no professional experience, I had a great editor. It makes a big difference, so pay attention (and you'll still be able to get paid while you learn).

What You Can Expect

If you have never written for a periodical, be aware when you are given an assignment you will also be given a due date and a word count. Whatever they are—*stick to them*. There is nothing more irritating for an editor than receiving a 2000-word article when he/she asked the writer for 800 words, or for a writer to deliver an article past the due date. Follow your instructions to a "T," make your editor happy and you will be the person that gets called again.

Since your assignment may require you to research information only available on Japanese websites or to interview a Japanese person, always ask if there's a budget to cover any translation/interpretation. In my experience, there never was. This can be frustrating because you can't get the information you need fast enough (unless you're fluent). I overcame this problem by personally paying for a translator or interpreter or by utilizing Google or other websites that do basic translations of Japanese text. (§ "Translation/Interpretation"). Note: A translator or interpreter need not be expensive, especially if you develop a circle of Japanese friends who are trying to improve their language skills. They may accept an English lesson in exchange for their services. Even if they don't, you will certainly end up learning some helpful Japanese words/phrases.

Helpful Hints

- After sending query letters, make follow-up phone calls. This is good sense any time you seek writing work.

- Don't overlook "easy English" magazines for beginning-to-lower intermediate English-language students (§ "Media"). You get paid the same as you would to write for a native English-language publication. Don't worry if you don't think the article represents your ability; your goal is to get published and paid.

- In tandem with the above, don't think that because you're writing for Tokyo-based publications that you don't have to worry about the quality of your writing. Now that most publications also have online versions, prospective employers can easily view samples of your work, so, make sure your writing sings.

ENGLISH LANGUAGE-RELATED JOBS

LYRIC WRITER

"When I found your sour milk in the fridge, I cried."

Writing English lyrics for Japanese pop (J-pop) songs is not as unusual a job as it sounds, though you can't make a living from it. Also, be aware that whatever you are paid for your English lyrics, it's almost always a "buy-out." Meaning: You will never be the official English lyricist of the song in question and will never receive future royalty checks from JASRAC (Japanese Society for Rights of Authors, Composers and Publishers, § "Media"). That said, it *is* possible to receive royalties under certain circumstances (see later this chapter).

"I Cry On Your Smile": How to Write English Lyrics for J-Pop

Shortly after having one of my original songs recorded by an American vocal group that was popular in Japan, the group's Japanese producer asked me to write English-lyric translations for several hit Japanese songs he wanted the group to sing.

As I could read music and *hiragana* and *katakana* (both used when writing Japanese lyrics for sheet music), I thought it would be a snap to whip up an English lyric based on the original Japanese. It was—after I attended several meetings where the producer would explain, in broken English, the deep, hidden meanings (sometimes bizarre, sometimes touching) of the original Japanese lyrics. Based on his notes, I plumbed the fifth dimension of my imagination to create lyrics that not only captured the meaning of the original lyrics, but (mostly) sounded natural in English, too. Over the years these lyric challenges have made me a much better writer as they opened my eyes to worlds of thought that would have never occurred to me. Here are the titles of some of the songs I've "redone":

- Peach-Colored Sigh (orig. *Momo Iro Toiki*)
- You're My Baby Red Sweet Pea (orig. *Akai Sūto Pī*)
- Returning Your Smile (orig. *Hohoemigaeshi*)
- From Bathroom With Love (orig. *The same!*)

Salary

There is no set fee for this type of job. I have been paid anywhere between ¥20,000 and ¥100,000 per lyric translation. Higher fees seem to be paid based on the popularity of the song being translated, the popularity of the vocalist or group that will eventually sing the translated lyric, and *possibly* the translator's ability and track record. Also, although this never happened for me, it is possible, as I mentioned, to receive royalties, under certain circumstances. See "Helpful Hints" below.

What You Need to Know

Because you are a native English speaker in Tokyo, you may eventually be approached by someone asking you to write English lyrics to a Japanese song. If they think you are naïve they'll ask you to do it for free, saying it will "only be used once" for a "special performance." Whether it's true or not, politely decline. Someone will be making money off your translated song—it just won't be you.

On the other hand, you may, as I did, receive legitimate offers to write English lyrics to famous Japanese hit songs of yesteryear. You will be given a rough translation of the Japanese song and asked to match in English, as closely as possible, the meaning of the original lyrics.

As mentioned, for each set of lyrics you write you will be offered a "buy-out" fee of between ¥20,000-100,000. You will almost certainly receive no other royalties. You may be offered a group of songs at once and if you get the high end of the above-mentioned fees, you might think, "Fantastic!"

Think again: You are being taken advantage of. What you are not told is:

1) Anyone can (and will) record a new version of the song using your English lyrics—and you won't get paid any additional monies for the use of those lyrics;

2) Since you are not the official English lyricist, anyone else can also write (and record) new English lyrics for the *same song*.

In other words, while a version of the song you wrote lyrics for will almost certainly be recorded and released, so will the other lyricist's version. You may also have the "added pleasure" of having your version recorded by an overseas artist who is only famous in Japan, while the other lyricist's version is recorded by a once-famous American pop star. You may also be "lucky" enough to hear the lyrics you wrote (and aren't receiving royalties for) being sung by the above-mentioned artists on Japanese radio. All this and more has happened to me.

If you want to break in to the Japanese music business and if you are told someone famous will sing the words you write, these job opportunities will sound tempting. I was given many of these opportunities and took all of them, even though I felt the payment was too low. Finally, though, after 10 years of doing this type of work, I was asked to write English lyrics for an album worth of songs made famous by a popular Japanese singer-songwriter. The songs would be recorded by formerly famous American pop music stars. The pay was definitely higher than I had received in the past, but still woefully low. Just the same, I gritted my teeth and did it, and now I can proudly say that Roberta (*Killing Me Softly*) Flack and Richard (*Right Here Waiting*) Marx, among others, sang my English lyrics. Will I do this kind of work again? No; now it's your turn.

What You Can Expect

Depending on your Japanese ability, you will either be given a rough translation of the original lyrics and/or a "lead sheet" (a simplified piece of sheet music showing the chord symbols, melody line and lyrics) with all the lyrics written in *hiragana* and *katakana*. If the person asking you to do the translation has any English ability, you are usually talked through the song and given an explanation of its meaning. Beware: The territory covered in J-pop songs is a far cry from the customary "I love you" or "You broke my heart" themes of Western pop songs. The images and storylines will take many of you aback; I suggest not trying to make sense of them. On the other hand, these images and storylines are sometimes deeply moving and may inspire you, if you ever decide to write your own original lyrics.

If you are asked to do this type of job, nine times out of ten it has to be done "immediately." I'm not sure why, but I think it's because the Japanese love to feel there is some sense of drama and urgency when doing creative projects. This gives them a chance to run around and look busy—and if you take this kind of job, you can, too! I managed to finish a set of translated lyrics in about two to three hours. If you are new to this kind of work, do not worry. If you've ever written a (rhyming) poem in English, you can write a lyric for a pop song.

Lastly, if asked to write English lyrics for more than one song on any particular album, you may only receive the credit "English lyrics by" once and be asked to use a pen name for any other set of English lyrics. I was told by a Japanese music producer that the Japanese people "won't like it" if they see that the same person has written all the translated lyrics. This practice has also spilled over to bylines for original articles I've written for Japanese English-language magazines.

Helpful Hints

- If you don't know how to read *hiragana* and *katakana,* now's the time to learn!

- Have a great E-J/J-E app at your disposal.

- *Sing* your translated lyrics along with the original Japanese version. Make sure the translated lyrics not only sound natural, but also that they match *every* syllable of the original.

- If an English word was used in the original Japanese version (most likely with a *katakana* pronunciation), use it in your translation, regardless whether you think it makes sense. If you don't use it, you will be told to put it back in so that it mirrors what is being sung in the Japanese lyrics. This may interrupt the natural flow of your English lyrics, but that's part of the challenge of doing this job.

- Make an effort, even if you think it will disrupt the *wa* (harmony), to ensure that 1) you are the official English lyricist for the song you have translated and/or 2) you will receive royalties for your English lyrics. While it is not impossible to achieve these things, the original composer and/or lyricist must agree to the above two items. If you feel this "status" or the royalties (which are limited as you are not the original writer) are worth pursuing, ask the producer of the album to contact JASRAC to attempt to negotiate these things for you. If neither the producer nor JASRAC is able to help, your only other hope is to track down the composer/lyricist or his/her representative, and plead your case. It may not result in tons of extra money, but in the long run it will be nice to know if the song is ever recorded in English again, it will have to be done with *your* English lyrics—as it should be.

❖

ENGLISH LANGUAGE-RELATED JOBS

TRANSCRIBER

"Today's guest [STATIC]… and [COUGHING] …"

Transcription jobs don't come up that often, but in my experience they have generally paid more per hour than other freelance jobs in Tokyo. However, beware: money is nice; sanity is nicer.

Salary

I have been paid anywhere from ¥10 per word to transcribe a 10-minute video to ¥60,000 to transcribe a 60-minute recording. Negotiate for as much as you can as you will often be given recordings of international conferences or shareholder meetings where native English speakers are few and far between, and, like the finest gold digger, be expected to sift through static, mic noise and people sneezing to discover shiny nuggets of words and phrases.

What You Need to Know

It is unlikely you will see classified ads for this kind of job. Most likely, you will receive transcription work while working for companies where you are already editing, writing or proofreading (but remember this also means you will only be paid your regular hourly salary to do the transcribing). In these cases, hopefully you will have access to software that will allow you to do your transcriptions with ease. In the event you are doing most of your freelance writing assignments from home, you may need to purchase such software, as transcription requires repeating passages multiple times. At the very least, make sure you have a great Internet connection for downloading the audio/video file that needs to be transcribed and some excellent headphones.

On occasion, the only format available will be a CD or DVD, so, make sure you have access to a CD/DVD player or a computer which plays CDs/DVDs so you can successfully transcribe the project.

What You Can Expect

You will most likely be asked to transcribe sound files of interviews with product manufacturers, company managers, the occasional movie star or, more likely, international medical/scientific conferences where, as mentioned, English is not always the speakers' first language.

With all of the digital technology available in Japan, there is no reason why these sound files shouldn't be crystal clear. However, for reasons that remain unclear, they often sound like they were recorded by some misguided individual standing too far away from his/her subject. It never seems anyone has ever taken the time to do a sound/volume/level check; on the contrary, the "record" button is pushed with the supreme confidence that some foreign transcriber (you) will be able to understand the (often inaudible) ramblings of whoever is speaking.

Because this type of work often requires you to replay short passages *hundreds* of times in hopes of capturing words and/or fragments of sentences, you should only agree to take on a project if what they are paying you is worth your while. If, after listening several times, you still can't decipher what's being said, type the words [UNCLEAR] or [INAUDIBLE]. Most companies who asked me to do this work were well aware of the poor quality of the recording and did not penalize me if I couldn't understand what was being said. Just do your best and hand it in. I promise you, if you were unable to completely transcribe the file, it will be given to another poor soul (almost certainly Japanese) who will be forced to sit up till dawn trying to figure out those inaudible words/phrases.

Helpful Hints

Don't get frustrated—which is easy to do if you must repeatedly replay sections to catch difficult passages. If you do this work often enough you will start to develop a "sixth sense" that sometimes can help you decipher the indecipherable.

❖

ENTERTAINMENT-RELATED JOBS

ACTOR/EXTRA/MODEL

"We have too many foreigners in this commercial. Could you pull your hat down so we can't see your face?... That's better."

(Actual quote from an interpreter on set of a commercial that I—and apparently too many other foreigners—appeared in.)

As many who come to Tokyo quickly learn, your "foreign" appearance and native English-speaking ability may be all you need to land good-paying jobs as an actor/model in Japanese TV commercials, TV shows and movies.

Because so many Westerners are aware of this (and have imagined their own brilliant stars lighting up the universe), Tokyo is now littered with as many wannabes as Hollywood. And just as in Hollywood, they learn what even top stars know: Directors don't know what they want till they see it. That said, I have not bothered preparing for any audition in Tokyo since it hasn't made any difference in my "career"—and I have averaged a commercial a year since coming to Japan. I have also been featured on the cover of a (health) magazine and have worked as an "extra" in TV shows, all based on the incredible training I received in my high school drama class, my Ben Kingsley-look-a-like face, or some other quality I have yet to figure out. Whatever it is, I have invested little time in pursuing these kinds of jobs and I have still been able to make a spare ¥300,000-500,000 a year, which suits me fine. You might want more—there may be more.

Making Faces: How I Became an Actor in Tokyo

The only acting I had ever done had been in high school. When I came to the conclusion I would never be a leading man, I gave up my dreams of winning an Oscar—until I came to Tokyo. Following the advice of the first foreigners I met after arriving, I registered with a few entertainment agencies. I never really thought they would call me. Wrong.

Within weeks I was asked to audition with other foreigners to act as excited bystanders at a horserace. I arrived with my agent and, after formalities were completed (see this chapter,

"What You Can Expect"), I was paired with a young French woman. We were asked to become hysterical with joy as we "watched" our winning horse cross the finish line. After much screaming and jumping, we were thanked and dismissed. I didn't give my audition a second thought—until I was called several days later by the agent who proudly told me, "You got it!" The next day I showed up at a real racetrack where I enthusiastically jumped up and down for the director and camera crew. For three hours work I was paid ¥100,000. Not bad for my first professional "acting" job.

Salary

Based on the information I received from all the foreign talent I spoke with in Japan, it seems there is no organization (such as the Screen Actors Guild in the United States) that ensures actors are paid appropriately and in a timely manner. However, in my experience, the following fees have been fairly standard:

- Movie/Television Extras: ¥10,000-20,000 per day
- Commercials (called "CM" in Japan): ¥100,000-400,000 per day
- Print ad Modeling (not high fashion): ¥20,000-150,000 per shoot
- Television programs which include English-language skits for ESL students: ¥25,000 per show

(A short description of each of these jobs follows "What You Need to Know" and "What You Can Expect.")

What You Need to Know

Agents

To work as an actor/model, you need an "agent." I put that word in quotes because while there are many agencies in Tokyo that represent foreigners, it's hard to know which are legitimate. You will quickly learn about these agencies from fellow foreigners, who, if they don't fancy themselves celebrities, might share contact numbers with you. Occasionally new or "regrouped" agencies will pop up on English-language sites. Call them and express interest in being an actor/model. You will be asked to come to their office and register your personal information (and, most likely, have a photograph taken of you). Some ask for a ¥1000 registration fee. Should you pay? I paid one agency and they gave me several nice jobs through the years, so I'm not complaining. Other agencies just have you fill out a form with your name, address, etc., as well as your measurements, including height, weight and clothing size for almost everything. Why? If you get a job in a CM or TV show, you will most likely wear a costume—and the agency wants to quickly provide your measurements to the client. Save yourself and them time and trouble by knowing what these measurements are. Note: The metric system is used in Japan. (§ "Metric Converters") Also note: None of these companies represent you exclusively unless you are a "big name," so register with as many as you want.

Photos

As in Hollywood, you need a good photo—but not Hollywood standard 8x11 headshots. Japanese agencies seem to prefer A6 (105 x 148.5mm) photos with four poses placed in plastic sleeves, stapled together to form a booklet. From these, the agency will choose the photo it likes best and send a copy (sometimes, inexplicably, a bad photocopy) to the prospective client. If the client likes this photo, you will get asked to audition. Note: Whether you have a professional photo or not, your photo will be taken (for free) at the agency. For reasons that remain unclear to me, this (free) photo often ends up being the one the agency sends out. Regardless, you may still need to provide them with the photos listed above.

Tell the Truth

In addition to photos, make sure to have a Japanese résumé (sometimes referred to as a "profile"). For those with no acting experience, list other skills (i.e. fluency in a foreign language, social dancing, etc.). When you meet with an agent, you will have a brief interview and be "assessed." Do *not* lie about anything (especially your visa status!). In other words, if you want to stretch the truth of your stint in a high school play as being an indication of your ability to act, fine. But if you tell the agency you have special skills (singing, unusual sports, etc.), you better be able to deliver. If they ask if you can do some challenging physical activity (horseback riding sometimes comes up), don't say yes if you really can't; it will just cause problems for everyone.

Time Commitment

In the past, none of the jobs described below ever lasted longer than a day or two. But things are changing and more foreign (usually Western) talent are being utilized. That said, only a lucky few will get a part in an ongoing/limited series. Everyone else will be relegated to commercials. In addition, while you might see a handful of fluent Japanese-speaking foreigners on Japanese TV on a regular basis, you will quickly determine they are 1) foreign language teachers who can explain the grammar of their language in Japanese; 2) commentators; or 3) token *gaijin* who end up on some kind of game show for the sole purpose of making the audience laugh.

What You Can Expect

Getting the Call

After registering with agencies, you will be called for auditions (sometimes right away), usually for commercials, but sometimes for TV shows, films or fashion shoots. You may also be called to work as an "extra." (See this chapter, "Movie/Television Extras.") The agents are often not able to tell you the time/location of the audition; however, they may be able to tell you the approximate dates of when the job will take place (with an extra day or two scheduled in case of rainy weather—*days they will expect you to hold*). You will be asked if you are available during this period. At this point, if they haven't told you the job location, ask if the shoot will be in Tokyo. They may not be able to answer, but be aware that some shoots require going out-of-town for overnight stays, and sometimes traveling to other countries. Your transportation and meals for any job outside of Tokyo should be paid for by the agent—but ask upfront and confirm that they are.

Availability/Restrictions/Payment

The time, date and location of these possible jobs should be carefully considered as you will most likely have already scheduled some other freelance job. *Tell the agent this information!*

Say you would have to readjust your schedule in order to do their job. They will take this into consideration and tell the client. If the job is a CM (TV commercial), you will also be told what the product to be advertised is and if there is a "restriction." This information, too, should be considered seriously. In other words, if you do a CM for a popular company's latest electronic marvel, you may be restricted from doing any other CMs for similar electronic products for a period of three-to-six months. If this is the case, your *gyara* (salary, or guarantee—a word used for entertainment-related jobs, not 9-5 office jobs) should reflect that. The agents may not know what the *gyara* is when they first call. Whatever the job is, though, I strongly suggest that you do *not* agree to do it until you know in advance what you will be paid.

If the conditions/*gyara* aren't acceptable or, more importantly, if you have already done a CM for which you have a "restriction," be honest. If you aren't, you will cause yourself and the agency untold problems. Your honesty ensures the agency can trust you (this doesn't necessarily mean you can trust *them*) and that you can attend the next audition without worrying about a restriction.

Photo Selection

Providing you with all of the above-mentioned information is really only a prelude to the agent asking if they can submit your photo to the client. This is a great opportunity for you to say "no"—so, again, carefully consider the job offer. (See this chapter, "Getting the Job—Maybe.")

Why would you say no to the possibility of a big-paying job? Read on and you will understand.

Within a day or two, assuming you've passed photo selection (you are called with an apology if you don't), you may finally learn where/when the audition will be held. You may also now be told (again) when the actual job will take place. At this point you must decide if it's worth rearranging your life for the *possibility* of appearing in a CM/TV show, etc. This can be extremely difficult if you have signed a contract to work for an English language school or have any other job that requires you to show up in person and at a prescribed time. (This is why I suggested earlier forming your own company of qualified substitutes to cover such situations.)

Assuming you have agreed to what the agent has presented, you are now ready for…

Auditioning

You will be given a time and meeting place (always ask to be sent an e-mail link to a map). Once you arrive don't be shocked when you see 50 other foreigners who are meeting the same or different agents, and who will attend the audition with you. There are lots of hungry *gaijin* in this town all searching for that pot of yen at the end of Rainbow Bridge in Tokyo Bay, and you will often see the same ones at every audition you attend. Once you get over the shock that you are no longer unique, you will follow your agent from the meeting place to the audition space. (Your agent will often stay with you to ensure that you follow the necessary protocol, and sometimes interpret what the director or casting agent wants when it comes time for the actual audition.)

In the audition space you will most likely be herded into a smoke-filled room where information sheets are being frantically filled out by the other agents who also represent foreign talent.

While you are waiting to be called, an assistant may take a picture of your face and full body shots. Unless you are used to smiling and posing in front of a camera, *practice your smile and pose in front of a mirror*. This might seem odd, but you will feel confident knowing how to smile and pose—important because the photo will only be taken twice: one face shot, one full body shot. Also, don't be alarmed if the camera is literally "in your face." Assistants are not pro photographers, so don't get your diva dust in a dither if you don't like how they snapped your mug.

Next you will be shown a storyboard (a cartoon-like drawing of what should happen in the CM). The agent or production assistant will walk you through it carefully. Don't be surprised if you are asked to speak or read something in Japanese. (I told you to study, didn't I?) Also, don't be surprised if you are asked to sing, fall down, make faces, scream, show your teeth, show your hands, run, act like a clown and other activities you probably haven't partaken in since your third birthday. You might also be asked to act as a waitstaff, bellhop or a long list of other "service people." Whatever you are asked to do, listen carefully. If you don't understand, ask until you do. If you are not a trained actor your best bet is to imitate *exactly* what has been described to you in the storyboard. From my experience, this is what they want (or what they *think* they want.)

When your name is finally called, you are ushered into the audition room, usually with your agent. (Note: You may be waiting an hour or more, so schedule this extra time and get over hissy fits in advance.) The first thing you do is politely greet (preferably in Japanese) whomever you meet. Note: You *may* be called in with a *group* of other auditionees. This is mainly done because of space limitations, not to embarrass you; the plus side is you can see how others handle the audition (unless, obviously, you're first), so listen and learn! Next, you are told to stand on a taped spot while holding up a piece of paper with your name, agency's name and other information about yourself (age, height, etc.). You are then asked to give a brief self-introduction—and often asked to do so in Japanese. If you can, great; if not, have someone write out a Japanese introduction or use phrases provided in this book (see "Helpful Phrases: Auditioning for an Acting or Modeling Job"). You'll then be asked to turn slowly as a camera records all sides of you for posterity.

Now you're ready for action. The director or assistant asks you to perform tasks deemed necessary to satisfy their curiosity. Be natural. If you aren't an actor, just try to capture whatever they ask for (it may not be easy). For reference see actor Bill Murray's true-to-life experience shooting the whisky commercial in Sofia Coppola's film *Lost in Translation*.

Most auditions follow this format. If your agent has his/her act together, you will be contacted by phone within a day or two with results. If you get the job, break out the champagne; if not, don't get angry, even if you've moved heaven and hell to rearrange your schedule. There are *no* guarantees in show business.

Getting the Job—Maybe

One reason I suggest teaching private English lessons is because if you pursue an acting career in Tokyo, you will quickly discover that auditions and potential jobs invariably fall on dates for which you have signed an unbreakable contract to teach English at some God-forsaken machinery company located 45 minutes outside the city. You could call in "sick," but this excuse grows old faster than you will living in Tokyo. If you call in "sick" more than once, the agency that hired you will not offer you other English-teaching jobs—*jobs you may need*. Why bother in the first place?

MOVIE/TELEVISION EXTRA

For those unfamiliar with this job, an extra is someone on the set of a film/TV show who fleshes out a particular scene. While the two stars kiss on a city street, everyone walking by is an extra.

You need no special skills to be an extra, but you must be able to follow instructions and have patience—lots of it. Expect to wait on set for *hours* before being asked to do something. You may also be asked to say something (usually incomprehensible English) or do something (bow, laugh, do pratfalls, etc.) that you may not want to.

To sustain you through this experience, you are usually given a meal, which is either a ¥500 *bentō* box or sandwiches on crustless squares of white bread. (Note: If you're a vegetarian, it's better if you pack your own lunch/snacks.)

If the shoot goes over schedule, you may get more money (and another *bentō* box), but don't count on it. You will, however, at least get taxi fare if you must stay past the last train. (Note: Most subways/trains stop running around midnight.)

The best/worst thing about being an extra is meeting fellow foreigners and comparing notes (or war stories). The first question is, "How long have you been in Japan?" This establishes whether you're a fresh-faced or jaded old *gaijin*. There is much to learn from both so keep your ears open, business cards handy and a smartphone ready for storing all the new contacts you'll make.

Note: Some people are reluctant to give up their hard-earned contacts; others feel the more the merrier. I was fortunate enough to meet a few from the latter group. Advice: If you prosper in Japan, don't be stingy. If you are that good, you will get the job. Meanwhile, if a fellow *gaijin* is scrounging for work, share a contact or two.

Being an extra is the bottom of the food chain for actors and it's my opinion not to waste your time (unless you are new in town and need to get connected). Focus on CMs, TV shows and modeling, and tell your agent politely you don't want extra work. They won't hold it against you.

CM (TV Commercials)

As with any other job in which foreigners are used, the pay for a CM may initially sound seductive. "Wow," you'll say. "One hundred and fifty thousand yen for a day's work? I'm there!" What you don't know is that, yes, it is *one day's work*. The Japanese seem perfectly willing to work a 24-hour shift, and will expect you to do so, too—without complaint. The main reason these CM take so long is no one seems to know what they are doing and/or the sets, staff and rentals are so expensive the job must be completed in a day. As such, these jobs force you to become patient and to give up any sense of your Western self. If you agree to the conditions and understand what you are getting involved with, then come to the set and do the job willingly and do not question things; accept them.

There are no guarantees you will ever be hired for another CM, but the Japanese staff who represent you will make a mental note of your attitude—so don't be a *prima donna* demanding a private dressing room, vegetarian meal or any other perks your inner celeb assumes it should have. When the stardust settles you may be back on the street tomorrow, interviewing at the "Pretty Kitty School of English for Toddlers" for a substitute position on Sunday mornings in August in a room without an air conditioner (or windows).

Modeling (non-professional)

These are usually one-off gigs for print work for posters, magazine ads, etc. When the agent says, "The client is looking for a model for their new brochure," they don't mean a long-legged stick figure with cheekbones and lip gloss; they mean you, the regular Joe/Jane who fits their image of what they want in their ad (apologies to the beautiful among you). You can get from ¥20,000-200,000 depending on what they expect you to do: i.e., stand at a podium like Evita for a newspaper ad, be the "non-hair" (bald) model in a health magazine, or play piano until a look of anguished passion crosses your face for a product brochure. (I did them all.)

These jobs are relatively painless and allow you to fulfill your fantasy of feeling special and beautiful. A qualified make-up artist is usually on hand to bring out the best in you.

NHK English-language-related programs

NHK (*Nippon Hoso Kyokai*, or Japan Broadcasting Corporation; § "Media") is Japan's sole public broadcaster and has been since 1953. As a public service, it offers several foreign-language education programs (filmed at NHK's Shibuya headquarters; § "NHK"). These programs are generally designed for Japanese children, young adults, travelers and office workers. If you hang out in Tokyo long enough, you too might be asked to participate in NHK's English-language education programs, which essentially feature cutesy role-playing skits, followed by helpful explanations from a bilingual Japanese teacher and a native-English speaking assistant. (Obviously if you are fluent in another language as well, more opportunities are available to you.)

For this type of work you can expect to be paid about ¥25,000 for whatever time you put in, which can be anywhere from an hour to an entire working day. Other than having a camera on your face while you speak grammatically correct English, there is nothing glamorous about participating in these programs. Of course, you can try posting a video clip for your friends and family to see, and possibly impress a few of your private students, but you would probably be better off filming yourself teaching your own class and uploading it to your website as an enticement to get more freelancing work.

The best thing that can be said about working at NHK is you will be able to experience what it must have been like to have worked in a communist country in the 1950s. Everything about NHK's headquarters is so staggeringly dull and austere it is only by a trick of light that the whole place isn't in black and white—including the people.

Unique Jobs

Anyone working in the Japanese entertainment business is sure to come across odd requests for one-off events, etc. I took a poll of fellow Westerners who had their 15 minutes of Japanese fame and culled a few notable *bon mots*:

- Singer/Choreographer, Female, 30s: "I had to choreograph six Japanese female dancers who had to dance on a float during a parade in Ginza. The float was about six feet by six inches, and the girls had to wear huge grape costumes (we were working for a wine company) which prevented them from lifting their arms higher than their elbows or kicking their legs higher than their knees. Their 'dance' was performed to the song *Volare*. It had to be seen to be believed."

- Actress, Female, 50s: "I was once asked to do a chipmunk voice for some computer game. I was specifically asked to eat nuts and make noises with my mouth and hands to get a 'real' chipmunk effect!"

- Actor, Male, 20s: "For a Halloween show I had to wear a 'character' outfit, get inside a cage and be carried around by another man dressed in a gorilla outfit. Don't ask."

Helpful Hints

- Agencies almost always contact you by smartphone, so make sure you *know your own phone number!* Lots of minutes have been wasted while people (including yours truly) have fiddled with their phones looking up their own numbers.

- On all the shoots I've been on there was always a highly qualified simultaneous interpreter on hand. You will marvel at this person (almost always a woman). Let it inspire you to improve your level of Japanese.

- When the job is completed, you will hear (and can repeat) that most beautiful of all Japanese phrases, "*O-tsukaresama deshita.*" (lit. "You must be tired," but here, "Thanks for all your hard work, the job is now finished.") This phrase is used for any situation where a great amount of effort has been used, but sounds particularly sweet when you finish an entertainment-related job. (Note: It is also occasionally used as a casual greeting.)

- Remember: Even if you're lucky enough to do a string of CMs or other movie/TV gigs, just as with other jobs in Japan, your pay will *never* go up—unless there are extraordinary circumstances such as overtime, travel to a foreign country or becoming a "regular" on a popular TV show (possible, but not likely).

- If you aren't a showbiz pro, remember: If you land a "high-profile" job (magazine cover, CM, "guest spot" on a TV show) and teach English part-time as well, don't bother telling your students about your brush with fame; generally, they will *not* be impressed. When you tell the Japanese, "I teach English," they do not take that to mean, "I also act, sing, dance and model on the side." If you're like most freelancers, you may find yourself running from a CM to teach an evening class. So, while *you* may find your "star by day, teacher by night" life fascinating, keep a low profile about it.

- Don't expect to get samples of your work. While some clients (i.e. Tokyo Gas, Fuji Xerox) post their latest CMs on their websites, most won't provide your agent with anything. Also, many agents refuse to trouble clients for copies of your CM or your voice jobs. Reality: You will use them to further your career by showing them to a new or different agency or even directly to a new client, so why should the (original) agents or clients care? However, it's not impossible; some relentless *gaijin* will absolutely not give up until they get their copy of a CM in which their disembodied head floats across the screen saying "Oh!" as a couple of Japanese children gorge on some kind of "healthy" chocolate biscuit. I say: If they show it on the internet, great; if not, don't give it any further thought and move on to the next job.

❖

ENTERTAINMENT-RELATED JOBS

HOST/HOSTESS

"Cheerful companions needed to light cigars. Must have college degree."

After careful consideration, I have decided that, while hosting/hostessing may qualify as a freelance job, things have changed too radically (in a negative way) since I first came to Japan for me to suggest pursuing this line of work. There are too many issues with visas, possible encounters with questionable individuals and no guarantee that anyone has your back. That said, I will list the basics required for this position, but with the caveat that *I do not recommend this kind of work to anyone* as a legitimate way to make money as a freelancer. (For further research, see: § "Host/Hostess")

First, hosting/hostessing is almost certainly reserved for Japanese men/women and/or for the rare foreign woman who meets a long list of requirements, which, in addition to requiring her to be beautiful and charming, may include the ability to speak fluent Japanese. For those unfamiliar with this line of work, suffice to say that hosts/hostesses are extremely attractive "companions" who work at clubs/bars where they pour drinks and light cigarettes for customers, engage in witty repartee and spend hours inhaling second-hand smoke. (I know this because I worked as a pianist in hostess clubs all over Tokyo; trust me, host clubs are the same.)

Salary

For a "standard" hostess job (pouring drinks, lighting cigarettes, engaging in conversation), hourly rates may often be the same as an English teacher's: ¥3,000. However, salaries differ depending on a club's location and clientele being catered to. Note: Many former high-flying clubs have felt the consistent sting of clients forced to cut back on "expense accounts," as well as the loss of customers to clubs offering strip shows, lap dances or more. As a result, salaries for "standard" hostess jobs are relatively low.

What You Need to Know

You must be young (18-25) and strikingly beautiful or handsome to get into the quality clubs. If this describes you, you have a chance in this strange world of *mizu shōbai* (the bar and entertainment business, a.k.a. "the water trade").

Because of problems with clubs who would illegally hire "foreign hostesses" without being concerned about their visa status, things that used to be easy (working in Japan on an "entertainer's visa") no longer are. If you have a spousal visa, permanent resident visa or you become a naturalized citizen, then your chances would be easier to get this kind of work... but if you had gone to that trouble to secure that type of visa, why would you be interested in pursuing this line of work?

For foreign men: opportunities are essentially non-existent. If you *really* want to be a host, one suggestion is to hang out in Kabuki-cho (the straight pleasure quarters located in Shinjuku; see § "Host/Hostess") and chat up the touts (the hardcore solicitors who try to snare customers) or go to Ni-Chome (the gay pleasure quarters, also located in Shinjuku; see § "Gay/Lesbian") and chat up the locals (both foreign and Japanese).

For either sex, my research indicates that being fluent in Japanese is required, whether or not you will be expected to use it.

What You Can Expect

As a hostess, you will be expected to light customers' cigarettes, pour their drinks and encourage them to buy more drinks—not to mention entire bottles of alcohol for the club to "keep on hand" for the next time they drop in (known as "bottle-keep"). You will also have to participate in conversations about their lives, pretend not to notice when they paw your breasts, dance with them (if space allows), all the while pretending you are charmed and fascinated by everything they say and do. You will usually work on some sort of rotation basis so that one customer doesn't get too attached to you—and vice-versa. However, you may get more money if you are requested by a customer. You will also be expected to cultivate customers and become their favorite, so that they come to the club often and spend as much yen as humanly possible.

As mentioned earlier, working at host/hostess clubs on an entertainer's visa is essentially a thing of the past. In the rare event that a club would offer you visa sponsorship, do *not* accept it. They will "own" you for the duration of your visa.

Helpful Hints

From my research, observations and experience working as a pianist in a hostess club, *I do not recommend hosting/hostessing for anyone.* Young women, in particular, can be taken advantage of horribly (and sometimes tragically) by seemingly "friendly customers." For those that feel this type of work is their calling in life, I again refer you to the *FIT* website (§ "Host/Hostess"), where you can find sites with more detailed information.

❖

ENTERTAINMENT-RELATED JOBS

MUSICIAN/SINGER

"I'm sorry, sir, but could you please not stick your baby's head in the piano while I'm playing it?"

If you are a professional keyboard player who sings and/or a professional singer, the following type of work is available:

- Performing in hotels/clubs/bars/restaurants
- Performing for weddings/wedding receptions
- Concert work (background singers/band members)
- Singing English songs for educational purposes
- Jingle (TV/radio commercials) singing
- Teaching music

If you play anything other than keyboards you might be able to find work backing a keyboardist or singer, but may fare better teaching private lessons or at a music school.

Don't Overstay Your Visa: How I Got My First Gig in Tokyo

Shortly after arriving in Tokyo I met a Brazilian woman who, after learning I was a pianist, told me to call her American friend, "the Piano Queen of Tokyo." I did; next day I had an audition at a major Tokyo hotel where a nervous Japanese agent, bassist, drummer and diva singer from the Philippines were waiting. The diva's pianist had overstayed his visa and was deported; they needed someone to start that night.

The diva liked me, the agent hired me, and I got an entertainer's visa and a job playing at the hotel six nights a week—which led to a string of other music gigs throughout Japan that have continued to this day. Lesson: Start networking from day one in Tokyo.

Salary

Salaries for musicians/singers have apparently been set in stone for at least the last twenty-five years:

- ¥10,000-15,000 per night to perform from three to six 30-45-minute sets (called "stages") at clubs, or ¥15,000-25,000 per night to perform at restaurants and hotels;

- ¥30,000-50,000 to sing one to three "stages" at a wedding reception, or a few songs during a wedding ceremony;

- ¥50,000 for pianists to accompany singers in concert (¥25,000-30,000 for sidemen);

- ¥10,000-20,000 per song to sing educational English songs;

- ¥4,000-5,000 an hour to teach at music schools (you teach in English—whether students understand is another question).

(Note: Jingle singing fees should be negotiated with an agent or a bilingual assistant, and they should be nice large chunks o' dough. As only truly qualified singers get hired for jingles, if you're at this level consider finding this kind of work in your own country.)

What You Need to Know

While you might think you can easily get a gig at one of Tokyo's hotels or clubs, some establishments only hire Western performers from abroad. This type of performer is usually offered a two-to-three month contract, all expenses paid, to do up to six stages (each usually 30 minutes in duration) a night, six nights a week.

That said, there are still many places that hire local foreign musicians. However, unless you have a personal connection to a hotel, club, bar or restaurant, the quickest route to music gigs is through an agent (see "Contacts"). Provide them with a professional photo, résumé (or "profile," mentioned earlier) and Youtube/website link to your performances. Note: The résumé need not be in Japanese, but it helps as agents usually translate them before presenting to a client. Take that step for them and be one step closer to work.

Your song list will also be requested. If you don't have one, don't bother moving forward until you do. And you should know (not fake) every song you put on the list, because the agents often forward that list to the client and you will be expected to perform those songs. So, think carefully what you put on the list. In addition, especially since I have done this type of work for the majority of my life, I find young singers in particular are woefully unprepared and have not bothered to learn or even be aware of standard songs. They also will not bother to learn songs requested by customers. This is a mistake and clearly marks them as amateurs. Singers: if you have not already, prepare a list of songs that covers jazz, pop, R&B and country standards. Also, familiarize yourself with songs made famous by Elvis Presley, the Beatles, the Carpenters, Billy Joel and almost any theme song from a Disney film. A *broad* song list will guarantee you the most work. Also, for singers: If you do not have the time, money or resources to have charts of your songs prepared in your key, *at least know what keys your songs are in (including "Happy Birthday")!* Since there are very few good Western singers of either sex in Tokyo, you will be at a distinct advantage as your charts will enable you to quickly work with Western/Japanese musicians—and you will be loved and remembered and called again because of your professionalism.

Lastly: Don't think that because this is Tokyo and not Los Angeles or New York that you don't have to be as good. I have worked with world-class singers and musicians in Tokyo. The competition has grown fierce over the years. So, come with your game on and you may find that your talents take you to places you only dreamed of.

What You Can Expect

While "non-smoking areas" in Tokyo's restaurants and hotels are more common than they used to be, they never seem to be where musicians perform. Hence, be prepared to encounter enough smoke to singe your lungs and cling to your clothing. If you are a non-smoker, your well-being is *never* a concern. I had to leave several well-paying jobs because of respiratory problems. If you're a smoker—dive right in; if not, have an iron lung on standby.

Do not expect, ever, that anyone will be listening to you or care about your performance. With the onset of smartphones, people may casually (or, more likely, rudely) snap photos or take videos of you in between their texts, but otherwise, the percentage of people who have an interest in what you are doing is minimal. Remember: Your purpose is to provide a "foreign flavor." At the same time, you will still be expected to be a professional entertainer—all while inhaling smoke and having your concentration trashed by people texting, chatting, snapping photos or shooting videos of you. There is *no* respect or concern..

Advice: Never perform a song you truly love and keep everything light 'n breezy. I got to the point where I'd play 50% bossa novas and 50% light swing tunes. By keeping everything bouncy, I never put too much of myself in any of the songs and was able to get through the night with a shred of dignity. If you haven't seen the film *The Fabulous Baker Boys,* do so now. When you see the scene with an oblivious waitress flipping on a blender as the boys start their first song, try to magnify that several (hundred) times and remember it when you start your own wonderful concert in Tokyo.

Helpful Hints

- Dancing/singing/performing customers: Do not be shocked if a drunk customer (always a man) comes up and starts dancing (or, worse, "singing") as you are trying to perform. Go along with it. Really, who cares? Most customers have been chained to desks for 12 hours having their souls drained from them by life-sucking companies who deny them any time to spend with their families; by the time they see you they are thrilled to still be alive. If you're a singer, try to keep them at arm's length. Pianists have it more difficult. The customer may join you at the bench. Remain calm. Just end the song quickly and take a break until the customer (or management) clues in.

- "Musician" customers: Some customers may also decide they would like to play piano (*with* you or while you are on break) or sing (*with* you or expecting/assuming you can play whatever it is they have in their fuzzy-logic minds). Be gracious and don't lose your cool. The management will almost always side with the customer. This is why it is important you *never,* under any circumstances, think you are a "star." If that's what you want to be, you're in the wrong country. If you are already a star, you aren't reading this book—unless it's for some laughs.

- Requests: Because you are reading this book, you will be sure to have a broad, extensive song list and be prepared to play the requests asked for. Nice tips? Sometimes. A standard tip is ¥1000, but on rare occasion, you can sometimes receive ¥10,000 tips.

- Unusual requests: Don't be surprised if you're asked to play "Amazing Grace" or some other off-the-wall song that wouldn't immediately be considered a standard request. This is because most "hit" songs in Japan are "created" by being featured in television commercials.

- Birthday Time: Regardless of where you might perform, if managers ask you to sing/play "Happy Birthday," they mean right that second or when they give you the cue. They do not care that you are in the midst of performing your brilliant acoustic version of Lady Gaga's "Bad Romance." You are expected to stop instantly or play in some kind of endless "holding pattern" until they give you the signal to play (and possibly re-play) "Happy Birthday" for the "surprised" customer.

- Meals: Many places I have worked at as an entertainer in Tokyo have provided me with a meal or, in the case of hotels, allowed me to eat in the employee cafeteria. The latter is generally unacceptable: you are expected to pay ¥500 for something that is sometimes inedible. Some people may not be bothered by eating the cheapest scraps that management can scrounge up and put in a *bentō* box—but I'm not one of those people. I have seen this type of "food" even at Tokyo's most glamorous hotels where you would think employees would be served a quality meal. Note: I have seen fellow foreigners get angry at the food servers because of the questionable quality of the food they are served; please do *not* do this. The food servers are given a limited budget to come up with something that resembles a meal—and that's what they have done. (They have to eat it, too.) Avoid troubling situations by bringing your own food with you.

- You also have the choice to "supplement" your meal by buying more food from vending machines that line the cafeteria's walls. The machines will sometimes carry thimble-sized containers of yogurt—but the rest tends to fall into a category I call "pastry-like substances." I found them inedible, but others were inhaling them as if they had been prepared by French chefs.

- Some hotel employee cafeterias are filled with smoke and the brightest, most irritating fluorescent lighting. There is also, on occasion, a TV playing full blast so it is impossible to do anything but listen to screaming "talents" on a game/cooking/sports show. I always spent my breaks elsewhere, even if it meant standing outside in freezing winter or sweltering summer weather for up to 50 minutes in between stages. Call me crazy, but when I take a break, that's what I want it to be. For others who aren't bothered by smoke, retina-scorching lights and deafening background sounds, the hotel employee cafeterias will suit you fine.

- Transportation: Some clubs/hotels expect you to play as late as possible and don't care that you'll miss your train and pay a third of your salary to take a taxi back home. This is wrong; make it clear to the agents that you need transportation money. Some will provide it, others (the ones that book you at five-star hotels and are making almost as much as you are in commissions) will state "there's no budget for that." I can say most certainly that that is a lie. If you feel you are being taken advantage of, it means that you are, so politely insist that they cover your transportation, unless the job is so fantastic that it doesn't matter (I can't imagine such a situation exists).

❖

ENTERTAINMENT-RELATED JOBS

VOICE ACTOR

"You want me to say what? But we don't say that in English... It's a new kind of English? Oh. I see."

If you are blessed with a pleasant, clear voice and good pronunciation you can find work as a voice actor in Tokyo. If you are truly good you may be able to make a living at it. However, the competition for voiceover work in Tokyo is fierce because it pays better than other entertainment industry jobs. If you decide to pursue this line of work you will encounter voice actors going behind agent's backs to get directly to clients, clients stealing voice actors from agents and everybody backstabbing and undercutting everybody. Be that as it may, go out and get yours!

Kickboxer Killer: How I Became a Voiceover Actor in Tokyo

Because I was always told I had a "character" voice when I lived in Los Angeles, I decided to take an expensive course that covered every aspect of the voiceover business. While the teacher confirmed I indeed had a "character" voice, I did not feel it had the quality required to be a successful voiceover actor—until I came to Tokyo.

Soon after arriving I met fellow Westerners who seemed to be raking in large amounts of cash doing voiceovers. When I heard their voices I thought, "If they can do it, so can I!" Though I had no professional credits, I knew how to put together a voice sample "reel" (see "What You Need To Know" below). I then answered every ad related to voiceover actors and let everyone know I could do voiceovers (though I never had). To my amazement, work started coming in. I can only assume it was because I was a native English speaker in Tokyo—not because I was a brilliant voiceover actor.

Fortunately my first voice job was with an experienced voiceover actress. We sat at a felt-covered table in a small recording booth and read some simple English phrases. I followed her lead and spoke more slowly and clearly than I usually did. I also spoke with a bit more enthusiasm (as she did). The client was happy; again, I got paid to learn.

This job led to many others, including ones where I finally got to use my "character" voice. Bizarrely, I was chosen amongst all the foreign talent in Tokyo to voice a video game kickboxing killer—who was Japanese! My "dialogue" consisted of the Japanese equivalents for "pow," "ouch" and "bash." Before we started recording, I simply had to ask the Japanese producers, "Why didn't you get a Japanese person to do this?" Their response: "We liked your voice." Lesson: Never question your talents (or what other people think your talents might be)!

Salary

While voiceover work was at one time extremely lucrative, there are now many hungry *gaijin* who work for less than the standard rate (about ¥15,000 per hour). So, if asked to work for less, I suggest you say no. If your voice has a unique quality, you should be paid accordingly. Reality: You may be recording something that will be used for years to come. Is it fair to be paid the same hourly rate as an English teacher to give a professional performance in a recording studio? No. When you hear: "That's all the client is offering," or "That's all we can afford to pay," be strong and say: "I'm sorry, this is my minimum." You'll be able to say this with confidence if you do enough of this work and start earning "serious" money, i.e. ¥150,000 to read a few lines of copy for a web/TV commercial; ¥200,000 to read the voiceover for a company video profile; ¥350,000 to do a few character voices for a computer game. Note: Regardless of what format your voice is used for, do *not* expect any residuals. As mentioned in "Lyric Writing" (see this chapter), payments for voiceover work, except in rare instances, are all "buy-outs."

When you are lucky enough to get voiceover work, please help maintain the standard of ¥15,000 per hour by *not* accepting less, whenever possible.

What You Need to Know

You must have professionally recorded voice sample files on your website or available to send via email, Dropbox or some other file-sharing service. If not, do not waste anyone's time pursuing this work. Your voice samples should not be more than five minutes in length and contain brief examples of the following:

- A passage demonstrating your ability to read advertisement copy. Read one slowly and one at a natural speed. Do *not* use a real product or brand name. Adapt existing copy and create your own names. (By doing so you will realize you can be a copywriter, as well!)

- A short news report with words specific to Japan (cities, geographical areas and Japanese cuisine are good choices) to indicate your ability to clearly pronounce Japanese words. If you like, include other general news events (international is fine) as well, but *adapt* them. Meaning: Do *not* discuss current events; your voice samples will quickly sound dated.

- A short one-point English lesson and/or dialogue that preferably features you and a member of the opposite sex.

- A numbered or lettered list of short phrases or vocabulary words (be sure to also say aloud the list's numbers or letters).

- Character voices for computer games, etc.

- If you are a professional singer, add a cut to show off those pipes.

- For DJs and emcees: include a sprinkling of (beautifully spoken) Japanese phrases.

Get to Know Your Agents

With your fantastic voice samples prepared, make sure any agent in town that handles voice talent is aware of your presence. Consider doing this by visiting their offices and handing them your *meishi* which has your website address on it. Let them know you have updated your site to include your voice samples, and that you would appreciate them keeping you in mind for any upcoming jobs. Your presence in their office, and offering a friendly hello, keeps you in the agent's mind more than if you just send your samples by e-mail. If you choose the latter, at least call to make sure the agent received it and to say *yoroshiku o-*

negaishimasu (a magical phrase in Japanese which means many things, but in this case: "Please consider me for future jobs."). Or, if this agent has gotten you work in the past, say, *"Mata, yoroshiku o-negaishimasu."* This translates something like: "Again, please consider me for future jobs, thank you." The clearer it is to the agent this is something you take seriously, the more you will be called for this kind of work.

The Audition

Once a year, some agencies take cuts from all of their voice-over talents' recordings and make a compilation of the sound files for their websites. From this compilation, potential clients can choose which voice best suits their project. This usually serves as your audition. However, you may still be asked to come to a studio and do a live audition. Unfortunately some unscrupulous clients only make it *seem* like an audition when, in fact, they are recording your voice for a final product! This is *not* common practice, but it happens. If you are at such an audition and it lasts longer than five to ten minutes, excuse yourself and speak to your agent (who may have accompanied you) and express your concerns. Explain that if the audition continues any longer than it reasonably should (five to ten minutes, maximum; perhaps slightly longer for character voices), you assume you will get paid for your time. The agent may also be surprised that the client is doing this, so don't jump to conclusions that they are in cahoots. Always be polite—but firm. Some agents have wised up to these situations and offer a stipend (from ¥10,000 for standard English conversation to ¥50,000 for product taglines) for auditions that they know may require extra effort on your part. At any rate, do your best and try not to get upset—but don't let them take advantage of you, either.

Know Where You're Going!

Once you have been selected for a specific voice job and the scheduled recording date/time are confirmed with your agent, *and* you have agreed upon a *gyara*, you are sent an e-mail link to a map of the studio location. This map may not be in English, so, again, learn the station names in Japanese (§ "Tokyo Subways/Trains"). If you are unsure about how to get there, have your agent's phone number and/or the phone number of the studio and be prepared to ask for directions (in Japanese) if you get lost ("Directions").

Study Your Script in Advance!

Usually a day or two before your recording session you will be e-mailed the script. You'll do a cursory glance of it and say, "A bunch of easy English sentences. No sweat." You'll forget about it until you show up at the recording session—only to realize the script contains: words you have never heard of, words you've heard of but don't know how to pronounce and grammatical mistakes that would cause *The Elements of Style* author William Strunk, Jr. to spin in his grave. As a result, you, unlike the other narrators in the room, will stumble over these words because you assumed you could do this kind of job "on the fly." Big mistake.

The client is counting on the fact that you, as a native English speaker, will know how to say the difficult words in the script. Learn them *in advance*. There are numerous Internet sites with sound files where you can hear correct pronunciations ("Reference"). Bottom line: Do your homework.

Also be aware the client may expect/assume you will fix screwed-up sentences. On the other hand, the client may *like* the screwed-up sentences as they are. All you can do is suggest that something does not sound natural. You will then be thanked profusely, or, more commonly, be given reasons why changes can't be made, the main one being the text you are recording has "already been prepared for publishing." In the end, you may end up saying bizarre combos that make no sense. Do not worry about your reputation. If they pay you to say "I eaten three apple yesterday night," just say it. As one of the top foreign voice talents in Tokyo told me, "I just close my eyes and think of Jesus."

Don't Be Late!

Always arrive at the recording studio a good ten minutes before you start recording. Once you start doing this work on a regular basis, you will quickly discover that if you rush to the studio from another job you will be winded, tired and/or stressed. This will show in your voice and will be a cause of concern for the client and/or reason for them not to hire you again. You don't want that to happen, *ever*.

What You Can Expect

You will most often be sitting in a tiny booth, alone or with another native English speaker (or speakers). The studio, depending on its quality, may or may not be air-conditioned. This is important when you consider the script you have been given may require anywhere from five minutes to six hours of recording time. (Breaks are usually every hour for longer recording sessions.) For those places without air conditioning, or places that turn off the air conditioning when the recording light goes on, there is absolutely nothing you can do except grin and bear it.

You will know it's time to start recording when a small red light, usually located on a nearby control panel, blinks once. On the same control panel you will also find a lever or knob that you can use to mute your voice when you need to cough (you will), drink water (you will), or trash your ex (you might). Advice: Be careful!

You will most likely record these kinds of things:

- Lists of English words, short dialogues, stories, quizzes, etc. The level of difficulty depends on who the recording is slated for: teens, college students, businesspeople, etc. (For dialogues, you may be expected to voice characters of different ages, so come prepared with three distinctive voices you can perform easily. Note: These voices are not the same as "anime/game character voices." See below.)

- Video promotions: Here you will be recording a script (anywhere from 5-20 minutes in length) for a video about a company's new product, with additional commentary on the company's history, accomplishments, etc. If you are hired for this kind of voiceover, it is likely the video has already been recorded with a native Japanese voiceover. If so, you will have a monitor so you can watch the original video and "follow along," either speeding up or slowing down certain lines to match the timing of the original. If you've never done this before, do not panic. If the producer of the recording session has his/her act together (and I regret to say, few of them do), you may be given the opportunity to listen to the Japanese version once so you can have an idea of how fast/slow to say something. If not, and if you are unsure whether to say something more quickly or slowly, you could say, *"Kono mama no supīdo de ii desu ka?"* (Is this "speed" okay?) Or *"Motto hayaku-shitari, osoku-shitari suru hou ga yokereba, oshiete kudasai."* (Please let me know if you would like me to do it faster or slower.)

- Anime/Game character voices: Anime is a Japanese abbreviation for "animation" and is on the growing list of Japanese words to have crossed over into the English language. Of any narration work you may receive while freelancing in Tokyo, anime/game jobs are the most fun. Remember: since you have demonstrated your versatility in your demo recording, the client may ask you to try a variety of voices on the spot. Have a few stock characters that you can pull out of your hat at a moment's notice. They should be distinct in tone, age and attitude. (Note: The fastest way to achieve—and remember—these voices is by writing down short descriptions of them. Carry this "cheat sheet" with you when you go to a job that requires you to do different character voices. Refer to the keywords in your descriptions and the voices should come to you quickly.)

Helpful Hints

If you have never done voiceover work before, prepare yourself by *slowly* reading *aloud* from periodicals on a daily basis. It is important to do this exercise slowly (and *daily*), as it forces you to pronounce things clearly and distinctly. Also, be sure to learn the meanings/pronunciations of any words you are unsure of. This simple exercise will demonstrate how challenging it is to actually read something aloud smoothly and clearly. Consistent practice will eventually pay off when you are able to walk into the studio, ace the job and impress the client.

❖

ODDS & ENDS

CELEBRANT
TEMP AGENCY JOBS
TRANSLATOR/INTERPRETER
WAITSTAFF/BARTENDER

For those in between hours…

CELEBRANT ("Celebrant")

I am not sure why this word is used to describe this job as the person doing it does not have to be a real priest, the ceremony over which he (in my experience in Japan, always a he) is officiating is not necessarily a religious one, and it is almost guaranteed he has no idea what he is talking about. Be that as it may…

To be a celebrant you must wear a priest robe (which you may have to buy) and recite speeches in Japanese at Japanese weddings. As it is possible to make good money in a relatively short time, it qualifies as a freelancer's dream for some; for others, it's a nightmare.

Salary

As there is now a glut of "foreign priests," salaries have leveled out. What used to pay ¥20,000-30,000 now pays ¥10,000-15,000 for each wedding (about 20-45 minutes) that you "officiate" at. Agencies representing celebrants will surely offer the lowest salary first. If you enjoy this work and become good at it, ask for at least ¥15,000-20,000. Alternatively, if your agent sees you've been doing a good job and has also received compliments from the bride or groom you may be offered a higher amount—but don't count on it.

What You Need to Know

First: This job is almost exclusively for Caucasian men (often in their 40s or 50s). Why? Perhaps the Japanese think this is what a Western priest is supposed to look like. Second: You must be able to speak Japanese in a way that does not offend the ear of a native speaker. You will be reading a romanized, Christian-influenced version of what a priest would say at a

Japanese wedding ceremony in front of two people who are actually being married—*by you*. In other words, they may have registered their marriage through their local *kuyakusho* (to make it legal), but, as far as a ceremony, *this is it*.

If you think you can pull off four-to-five weddings on a Saturday without breaking a sweat, perhaps this work is for you. But if a little voice in your head starts shouting, "But I'm *not* a priest," think carefully before you agree to do it.

What You Can Expect

You are given a script (written in *rōmaji*) in enough time that you have a chance to practice it. *Do so!* Even if your Japanese-speaking ability is good, the script uses special words and phrases reserved for the wedding ceremony.

Before the ceremony you go through a rushed rehearsal. *Be crystal clear as to when you are expected to read specific passages.* An agency representative will most likely accompany you (at least the first time) to ensure you don't mess things up.

When it comes time for the ceremony, you don a heavy embroidered robe, take your place on the pulpit and, voilà: you are now the priest who will guide the trembling twosome before you through their vows—all as a sea of Japanese faces stare at *you*.

To add to your heightened sense of awareness, your oratory may be "enhanced" with sounds of a Japanese "gospel" choir. While gospel is not the rage it once was in Japan, there remain some hardcore believers who will also don robes, stand on risers and wail in the background as you try to get to the end of your presentation without passing out from fear, shame, embarrassment—or all three.

There are some who think this is a blast; others (like me) will be tossing their scripts (if not their cookies) and running for the nearest confessional (or cliff) the moment they finish.

Helpful Hints

Thoroughly study your script (*especially* the names of the bride and groom) and practice in front of a mirror or ask a Japanese friend to check your pronunciation. For whatever reason the Japanese have decided they want a foreign priest, if you do this job, be loving and respectful of the people getting married. This may be a quick ¥10,000 for you, but this is the most important day in these people's lives.

❖

TEMP AGENCY JOBS ($ "Temp Agency Jobs")

You will occasionally see ads for temp agency jobs that require the skills of a native English speaker (although that person will often be expected to be bilingual). Depending on your language ability, salaries can range from ¥2,000-6,000 an hour.

Some agencies have websites that allow you to register online. Do so and start applying for positions immediately. If you have windows of time you would like to fill with short-term assignments (which sometimes lead to long-term assignments or higher-paying positions), temp agency jobs may do the trick.

Note: Because I had a Japanese résumé, temp agencies often contacted me for work. I eventually ended up teaching private lessons to the high profile president of one such agency, where I was also offered additional teaching work. The point: a Japanese résumé can prove invaluable, so get yours ASAP.

❖

TRANSLATOR/INTERPRETER ($ "Employment Opportunities")

If your language ability is such that you are capable of doing this kind of work, especially in challenging fields (i.e. legal, medical, etc.), you can call the shots as to what your rates are (top J-E simultaneous interpreters can command upwards of ¥20,000 an hour). My only advice for you here is to not join an agency. You will experience similar problems to those of entertainers: You get a set fee (usually low) and you will have trouble negotiating upwards.

There is always a need for a qualified (J-E/E-J) translator and/or interpreter in Japan, and there is always competition, so don't be surprised to bump into any number of highly qualified bilingual Westerners all seeking the same job. Again, *market yourself* (with a well-designed J-E website featuring your résumé and photo and bypass all agencies, middlemen and potential competitors.

❖

WAITSTAFF/BARTENDER

You might be surprised to know that there are many foreigners who work as waitstaff or bartenders in Tokyo. Sometimes these foreigners are hired to "enhance" the "atmosphere;" sometimes they are hired out of necessity. In either case, those of you who seek this type of work will most likely have to speak not only English and Japanese, but, in the case of restaurants that feature a cuisine from another country, the language of that country, as well.

As elsewhere, waitstaff/bartender can be a part-time or moonlighting position, or just an occasional fill-in job for special events. Salaries generally fall between ¥800-1,300 an hour and, if you weren't already aware, there is no tipping in Japan in restaurants/bars. (That doesn't mean you won't get any.)

While doing this kind of work may not make you rich initially, it is possible you might end up working for a Japanese entrepreneur who will open his/her own restaurant and decide to bring you along for the ride as a maitre d' or manager. Alternatively, you may team up with a Japanese (or non-Japanese) colleague and open your own wonderful restaurant/bar. So, if the restaurant business appeals to you, this kind of work may be appropriate for your freelance adventure.

ENTREPRENEURIAL ENDEAVORS

YOU ARE AN ENTREPRENEUR

Yes, you are.

You are young and smart. Or maybe you're old and smart. You've always known or sensed that working for someone else is not the path for you. You have some crazy idea to start your own business. And what's even crazier: you want to start it in a foreign country where you don't really speak the language and have no idea whether anyone will want what you have to offer.

You take a good look in the mirror. Scared, but unshakeable faith that you will succeed, you take a deep breath, and…

Go For It

The longer I've lived in Tokyo, the more I've seen people taking charge of their own destinies. This may entail creating actual careers, which doesn't really apply to freelancing. However, freelancing may lead you to realize that you actually have something to offer the world on a grand scale. As such, I've decided to at least touch upon this topic.

Going beyond "Teaching Your Specialty" (see earlier, this chapter), you are not only special, *you are unique*. This may have everything, or nothing, to do with you being a stranger in a strange land. Whatever that quality is that sets you apart, capitalize on it.

I have seen people turn passions for photography, filmmaking, singing, acting, blogging and more into great opportunities for themselves. Sometimes these individuals have teamed up with Japanese friends or spouses, sometimes with foreign friends or spouses, sometimes they go it alone. They have an idea, they figure out how to market it, they get a client or two, they roll that into other opportunities, and before they even realize it, their entrepreneurial visions are being realized.

I have worked for and with many of these people. I'm extremely impressed by their ability to not let language, culture, or anything else having to do with living in a foreign country stop them from achieving their goals. If that's you, again, go for it!

But, you ask: Is there really room in Tokyo for another media company or dialogue coach or talent agency or self-made singing sensation? Of course there is; the secret is figuring out how to market yourself and creating your own opportunities.

How Do I Get There From Here?

If you have been carefully reading this chapter, you have picked up numerous tips on how to market yourself. I think a few bear repeating:

- Set up a bilingual website which has a portfolio of your work. (If you don't have a portfolio, *create one*.)

- Always have your classy, glossy *meishi* which features your photo or some icon/design indicative of your company.

- Become a social media maven.

- Have a simple launch party for your business at a local bar or restaurant. Don't be afraid to ask people to pay a realistic fee to enjoy some food and drinks. Have a comic, a singer or an up-and-coming celebrity be your emcee for the night. Do a presentation. Show your passion, share your portfolio, make sure the audience knows how you or your company stand out from the rest.

Being an entrepreneur in Tokyo really isn't any different from being one in another city. One must think outside the box, one must have something to offer that will connect with the public, one must know how to present oneself and one's ideas, one must have a command of social media. If you truly have the dream, desire and drive, Tokyo can be a fantastic place to take a chance and make your mark.

Helpful Hints

If you do not know how to dress to impress or speak in front of the public, then get lessons in both. I have seen people fail because they thought that the thing they had to offer was so "cool" that they, themselves, did not have to make that much of an effort. Wrong. Pay attention to how others have achieved their entrepreneurial success and follow by example... then break the rules and create your own special world.

❖

IMPORTANT STUFF

GETTING PAID
HOW TO MAKE THE BIG YEN
SAVE YOUR MONEY
AND DON'T FORGET...

Go get yours!

GETTING PAID

Of all the things that will drive you insane in Tokyo, getting paid for your work as a freelancer is near the top of the list. This generally only applies to entertainment-related jobs, and specifically to voiceover jobs. There are any number of agencies that seem to think it's okay to pay you six months after the fact, if not a year. You must work hard to guarantee this doesn't happen.

One reason for confusion about payment may be cultural. I've been told by Japanese colleagues (and have read in various reference books) that the Japanese do not like to discuss salaries. There is, apparently, a philosophy that not only should you be grateful for whatever amount you are paid, you should never be *urusai* (noisy) about asking how much or when you will get paid. This "philosophy" may work for others, but not for me.

As for payday: In Japan each company seems to have a different payment schedule. Example: If you do a job on any given day of the month, companies (business or entertainment) will pay on the 5th, 10th, 15th, 20th, or 25th of the following month, or, more likely, on the last day of the following month. Some pay on the 5th of the *second* month following the job.

Some agencies, specifically those that handle voiceover artists, take three months or more to pay you, often giving the excuse that they never know when the client will pay *them*. Because they live in deathly fear of offending the client, all they can do is wait until the client pays. This is insane. You did the job; you should get paid in a timely manner. Others may disagree, but I suggest sending "payment reminders" to these types of agencies as often as possible until you get paid.

Now that you are aware of these "payment schedules," it is incumbent upon you to confirm upfront what your *gyara* is for the job and *when* you are to be paid. If you don't, many agencies won't tell you. I'm not sure why, but it's been my feeling that this is their way of paying you less than they're supposed to and/or paying you when they get around to it/feel like it. What are you going to do? Sue them? To my knowledge, there is no union to protect foreign talent in Japan. Many of these agencies have wised up and immediately tell you what you want to know, because they are aware that most foreign talents get *urusai* if they are not paid fairly and/or on time. This is good; still, there are any number of situations where agents will not bother to give you details unless you ask for them. It isn't right or fair, but it's reality—so be prepared for it. (Note: It is the agent/agency that pays you, not the client. If you do a commercial for Apple, Apple pays your agent/agency and they pay you. You will most likely never know how much a client is really paying the agent for your "foreign talent.")

When the agent finally breaks down and gives you the payment information you request, *write it down*. And, if you're like me (and you possibly risk alienating the agent if you do this), send them a confirmation e-mail with that *same* information (or request such from them) so they can't lie to you when it comes time for payment. On occasion, certain agents straight-out lied to me, saying the payment date was a month (or two) later than what they originally told me. If you think you're going to get work from this agent/agency in the future, you might have to grin and bear it the first time if they fudge with the payment date (not to mention the amount); but for every job they offer after that, e-mail them a confirmation (or request the same from them) so they don't get any funny ideas about not paying you on time.

In addition to the above e-mail, after you have completed your job, e-mail an invoice to the agent—but only if you sense there will be issues in the future. (Alternatively, the agent may request that you send them an invoice—always a good sign.)

I do not want to paint a grim picture of evil agencies hoarding your money until you have to hire a team of lawyers to get it (which, of course, you'd never do because [1] you couldn't afford it; and [2] by the time your case came to trial in Japan you'd be dead). Many agencies do pay what and when they say will. But if you haven't gone to the trouble of confirming the things mentioned above in advance, you may have issues getting paid. (Note: Once you have developed a working relationship with an agency and a level of trust has been established, it isn't necessary to e-mail a confirmation—but it is still advisable to confirm the job details/payment, at least on the phone.)

There are some foreigners in Tokyo who have had such experiences and have learned, like you will, that some agencies are better than others. You will hear soon enough by word-of-mouth which ones to avoid. Unfortunately, many people carry grudges, so you shouldn't judge an agency based on one person's opinion. I have listed (without judgment) agencies in the "Contacts" chapter I have personally worked for that have paid me in a timely manner, as well as other agencies that fellow Western talents have worked for. There are also some links on the *FIT* website to others (🔗 "Talent Agencies), although I can't confirm their legitimacy.

Other important points: Whatever *gyara* is quoted to you is usually the "before tax" amount. This means the agency will withhold 10% of your earnings. For example, for appearing in a CM, they may quote the before-tax amount as ¥200,000 yen (meaning approximately ¥180,000 after tax). This can make a substantial difference on larger jobs. Sometimes the agency will be willing to negotiate the *gyara* so that the quote they give you includes the taxed amount (i.e. the *gyara* is ¥222,222, meaning you receive approximately ¥200,000 after tax). Always negotiate to ensure you are paid the amount they initially quote you—not the "after-tax" amount. (👂 "Getting Paid")

Also, when the agencies do finally pay you, they don't have any compunction about deducting a "transfer fee" from your salary. This fee (which varies depending on how much money is being transferred) is an amount the bank automatically deducts when money is transferred to another person's account. (You will hear either *furikomu*: to transfer, or *furikomi*: a transfer.) This can be avoided by adding in the transfer fee when the amount is transferred, but most agencies don't bother to. Some agencies are aware this bothers foreigners and will pay you the exact amount they promised—as they should. On the other hand, you could (as some agencies suggest) open up an account at the exact branch where the agency has its account. This means you may end up having five or more bank accounts throughout Tokyo to accommodate each of your agents. This is a waste of your time and energy. You should be paid what was promised to you and it is my strong feeling that it is up to the agency to cover the cost of the transfer fee, not you. Bottom line: Politely clarify payment information in advance and you should get your full payment in a timely manner.

What Others Have to Say

- Singer/Actress, Female, 50s: "It once took me more than six months to get paid for an acting job. I was told the talent didn't get paid until the agency did. Another company I've worked for has to be constantly 'reminded' to pay me on time. My advice: Keep all the details they give you about the job (dates, times, payment amount, names, etc.) or some agencies may claim you never did the work for them."

- Writer, 40s: "Sometimes magazine publishers will 're-use' your articles on the magazine's website or in 'sister' publications—without ever notifying you. Unless you signed an agreement to the contrary, make sure when you agree to write an article for a publication that you are clear on how the publisher plans to "re-use" said article and whether you will receive any additional fees for it. Some publishers will contact you in advance to let you know they would like to re-run your article and that they are willing to negotiate extra compensation. Still, I would ask first in case they 'forget.'"

- Actor, 20s: "An industrial shoot I was working on with several other foreign actors went into overtime. The sponsor didn't want to pay for the overtime and reneged on paying the agency. The agency didn't want to pay the actors and I had to hound them for months to get my money. I am now with a management company which pays me monthly and deals with the agencies, sponsors, etc."

- Voice Actor, 30s: "I'm still waiting to be paid for a job I did years ago. A company associated with the project took off with the money. The agency I worked for is now involved in a lawsuit to get it back. Will I ever be paid? Fat chance."

If you want unions and lawyers to protect you, go to major entertainment cities like Los Angeles or New York; if you want experience in the entertainment business and the chance to make a spare ¥500,000 or more a year acting out your dreams, Tokyo might give you that opportunity. If you do get a chance to strut your stuff, do *not* let it go to your head or assume it means anything in terms of a "career." Remember: You are an English-speaking foreigner, or even a Japanese-speaking foreigner, and, except in rare cases, the Japanese entertainment industry considers you a unique accessory, something amusing and/or an atmosphere person.

If you approach the Japanese entertainment business with a light touch and try not to take it too seriously, you can have fun, learn a trick or two, earn some decent money and, most importantly, gain the knowledge that you can do just about anything.

❖

HOW TO MAKE THE BIG YEN

The secrets to making a great salary as a freelancer in Tokyo are not much different than those for freelancing elsewhere. However, knowledge of some "special" secrets will put you ahead of the competition. Let me share with you what I've learned the hard way:

- **Have a flexible schedule**. If you foolishly sign on to teach English for 25 hours a week with classes in the middle of the day, you will never have a schedule that allows you to accept high-paying (¥100,000-400,000) CMs or voice jobs—which often take place at a moment's notice.

- **Make networking a way of life.** *Always* carry your *meishi*—**the ones with a picture of your smiling face**—and whenever the opportunity arises (which will be often), hand them out. A *meishi* with a photo (not everyone has such a *meishi*) continues to work for me as it obviously helped jog people's memories when they called me for possible jobs. **More importantly**: When a Japanese person gives you their *meishi,* they will most likely say their name and their company's name. If the card has no English, and if you can't understand the person's name, *ask them to repeat it until you do,* make a mental note of it and write it down as soon as you can afterwards. Don't expect to show the card later to a Japanese friend and have them tell you the name (though they will be able to read the address). *Kanji* used in names sometimes have unusual readings even the Japanese can't always recognize. Once you have this information, enter it into a database. *This is essential!* You will meet so many people during your freelance adventure that if you fail to input their names/numbers into your database, you have lost a potential client (even if at that moment you don't know how that person or his/her business could benefit you).

- **Be willing to work seven days a week, day and/or night.** I don't mean not to sleep; I mean make yourself available—and say yes to as many jobs as you can. Be the person willing to teach an English class on Sunday while everyone else is sleeping off Saturday night's hangover (which, of course, you won't have, because *you* will have been working!); rewrite a grammatically-challenged business letter for your Japanese neighbor on your one night off (then later find yourself being introduced to his son, who owns a multi-billion yen corporation and requires a native English speaker to personally assist him at the office); be willing to travel a little further than others to do a proofreading job (then find yourself traveling with the company president to another country because he feels shaky with his English). Before you know it, you will be balancing three to four jobs a day and your bank account will grow exponentially.

- **Stay in touch with your agents/clients.** As you would elsewhere, make sure to send thank-you notes after important jobs and always send holiday greeting cards. For agencies which handle foreign talent, sometimes dropping by to say hello while dropping off a new picture, voice CD or DVD of a performance will keep you fresh in the agent's mind the next time a big job comes up. I also found that calling people I had worked for in the past (but had not worked for in a while) and asking them out for coffee and a chat was a great way to reconnect. Another way to keep your name at the top of the list is to send a simple gift (it need not be expensive; fruit or candy will do) during the *o-chūgen* (mid-summer gift) and *o-seibo* (end-of-year gift) periods. You should do this for as many of your agents/clients as you can, *whether or not* they provided you work within a certain period. You will learn that sometimes months go by before you get called to do a job; if you've been the person who has stayed in touch and your client suddenly gets a windfall of work, you, again, will be on top of the list.

- **Don't get too comfy once you start making money.** If you make the assumption the cash flow will go on forever, one day you'll awake to find all your freelance work has vanished—with nothing on the horizon for weeks or months to come. This is when you send friendly notes to people in your database, letting them know you are available to teach, write, etc. During one of my roughest periods, I contacted everyone I had ever worked for in Tokyo and in a matter of months, I went from making zilch to ¥800,000 a month.

- **Learn Japanese!** My biggest mistake in Japan was assuming my "daily conversational" Japanese was enough. *Chigaimasu, yo!* (Wrong!) Whether or not you will stay in Tokyo (or anywhere in Japan) for the long haul, put in your hours and study Japanese; the day will come when a wonderful job opportunity arises—and *you* will be able to take it because you followed my advice.

❖

SAVE YOUR MONEY!

More than once I walked away from 70% of the jobs I had—only to be able to return to all of them a year later. I'm not sure why I had this kind of luck, but, as mentioned: if you put some effort into nurturing your contacts, you will at least have someone you can call if and when all other work suddenly evaporates. If, however, you do not nurture those contacts, I have one word of advice: **SAVE**.

Shortly after getting my work visa, I was making, with the combination of jobs I landed, about US$7,000 a month. I was shocked considering I was killing myself with two full-time jobs to earn about US$3500 a month in Los Angeles. But like many people, now that I had money for the first time in my life I wanted to burn it—and did. Tokyo is a huge candy store beckoning you 24 hours a day, and there are any number of reasons to justify spending your yen:

- I'm working too hard and need to pamper myself.
- I've never had this much money—and may never again.
- Finally I can impress that new guy/girl!
- I'm going to make my dumpy *apāto* into a real *manshon*!
- It's expensive, but, hell, it's Tokyo—what do you expect?

I am not going to play the role of your miserly uncle who insists you pinch every yen and roll it up in your *futon*. However, I *insist* you have some sort of savings plan—preferably one which doesn't allow you to touch your money for extended periods of time. There are many sad-eyed *gaijin* in this country who have been here for 20 years and are *still* proofreading badly worded documents at ¥3,500 an hour (or less), because, *oops,* they forgot to save!

I know this should be elementary, but when people suddenly start making money, most don't know what to do with it. If you have never budgeted your funds, this is an excellent opportunity. Learn from error: If I had budgeted or saved with any sort of intelligence, I could have easily socked away $250,000 in 10 years or less—all from working the freelance jobs I have described in this book. While I fortunately saved something, it could have been much more. So, please: think carefully about your money. While it may be rolling in this month—and perhaps for the next several years—freelancing jobs can disappear without any apparent reason. I don't want to meet you on the street one day and hear you say, "You told me to save but I didn't listen, and now I'm busking for tips at night and teaching English to screaming toddlers in the morning."

Take the opportunities you get in Japan, let them help you grow financially, save—and save again—and you will be happy you did.

❖

AND DON'T FORGET...

I wrote *FIT* to help you achieve your financial goals, and I believe you can—by working hard, accepting as many jobs as you can and, as mentioned in "Making the Decision," *having goals*. It is easy to get distracted in Tokyo by all the goings-on and lose track of your goals; promise me you won't. Your goals might change, but before they do, *write them down* and keep them near so you always have a defined purpose while you live/work in Tokyo.

And...

For almost any freelance job you do in Tokyo, you are most likely getting paid more than your Japanese counterpart. So, while you may start making some "nice" money, don't complain in a few years when your salary remains the same. Just look over at your Japanese co-worker, who is probably putting in hours of unpaid overtime and trying to live on a salary that also has not risen in some time. Be cheerful and keep things in perspective—

and your experience as a freelancer in Japan will be a positive one.

And finally…

How do you keep the music playing? In other words, how can you keep the money coming in even after you've left Japan? Many freelancers, including myself, have been able to parlay their Tokyo jobs into continuing work in their own countries, including translating, proofreading, event planning and more. If you are able to make some solid contacts *and make the effort to keep in touch with them even when they don't have work for you*, you may be rewarded down the line in ways you cannot imagine.

THINGS YOU SHOULD KNOW

An A-Z of what you may encounter on your FIT adventure

As might be expected, Tokyo offers its fair share of "culture shock moments." Some will enchant; others will disturb. Following are some of the moments that I have experienced. Awareness of them may make your transition to freelancing in Tokyo a bit smoother.

AIR CON (*ea-kon,* air conditioner)

In Japan, the air con is essentially a little beige/grey box that has been or will have to be affixed to one of the walls in your place of residence. It is usually placed near the ceiling, in a corner. The problem is you will need one for every room in your home as, generally speaking, in most apartments there is no central air/heating. For those of you who plan to live in a one-room apartment, you're set; for everyone else, I suggest spending the coldest/hottest days of the year at your local Starbucks. Let them pay the utility bills while you stay cool/warm enough to plan your day.

AKIHABARA ("Electronics/Appliance Shops")

Also known as "Electric Town," this area is popular with tourists and locals alike as the place within Tokyo to buy electronic goods, appliances, etc. Although I have been to Akihabara many times, I find there is no advantage of going there over other major electronics stores such as Yodobashi Camera and Bic Camera (all located in Tokyo's major shopping areas in Shinjuku and Shibuya, as well as in Akihabara), all which sell the same products at comparable prices.

With some effort, you can usually find an English-speaking salesperson to assist with your purchase at any of the above locations (note: it may not be possible to receive an English-language manual for your purchase). But what Akihabara does not offer, which the above stores do, is a "point card." If you make frequent purchases of printer cartridges, paper, storage media, etc., at Yodobashi or Bic, the point cards you receive from them will fill up quickly and you'll be getting that pricey printer cartridge for free in no time.

AN

This is not an indefinite article—not in Japan. *An* or *anko* is a sweet red bean paste the Japanese worship. The Japanese, especially young women, have recently embraced an embarrassing riches of Western-style sugary sweets. That said, when push comes to shove, they love their *an*-filled confections. At first you might not be able to enjoy them; as time goes by you will be able to tolerate, if not appreciate, the subtle flavors and unusual textures. More importantly, you won't be able to escape *an*, no matter where you go. It shows up in everything, including being stuffed into otherwise innocent-looking breakfast rolls. Make sure you read food packaging labels carefully.

APĀTO

As discussed in "Getting Set Up," *apāto* are Japanese-style apartments in older buildings. They often have *tatami* mats for floors and *shōji* screen doors for dividing rooms. The bathroom is often separated into a toilet room, which may have a Japanese-style (squat) toilet, and a bathing room, which will most likely have a small, square tub, not a shower. While walking across *tatami* in summertime is cool to the feet, I find there is little else to recommend about *apāto*. When you begin your search for a place to live, try to secure a *manshon*, which is definitely more modern and will have a Western toilet. Smaller *manshon* have "unit bathrooms" which contain the bath/shower, sink and toilet; larger *manshon* have separate rooms for the toilet and the bath/shower.

BANKING

There are a few things you need to be aware of so you can handle your banking chores in Tokyo without having a breakdown.

- Checking accounts, individual or joint, are essentially non-existent in Japan. Most money deposited, withdrawn, or transferred is all done via ATMs and *furikomi* (electronic bank transfers, mentioned earlier) at your bank, other banks or convenience stores. (Note: ATMs in these establishments have limited English instructions.)

- As for a *futsū* (regular) savings account (which should be called a safe deposit box, because you will rarely see anything resembling interest in it): As your savings account passbook will show the *katakana* version of your name, verify the *katakana* spelling with several Japanese acquaintances. The reason: The bank may determine what the "appropriate" version of your name is. This may prove to be a problem later if their *katakana* and yours do not match. My name, David, is a perfect example. It's been spelled *deibuiddo, deibido* and *deibito*. This becomes a problem when people must transfer money to your account and there is a discrepancy in the *katakana* spelling.

- The bank may type, in English letters, your English name as listed on your passport and or *gaikokujin tōroku-shōmeisho* (alien registration card) on the cover of your passbook and then put the *katakana* spelling of your name on the first page of your passbook. To avoid problems, bring a bilingual Japanese acquaintance with you when you open your first Japanese bank account to help clarify exactly how the bank plans to handle your name and the *katakana* spelling of your name.

- As of this writing some branches of major banks *may* require you to have a *hanko* (a name seal that is made of wood, bone or plastic) to open the account. This is not difficult to obtain. You can usually find a *hanko* shop in your neighborhood; if not, ask someone at your place of employment to help you find one. You need not spend more than ¥3-4,000 yen on a *hanko* to have the *katakana* spelling of your name (usually your last name is fine) carved into it. Be aware the price may be determined by the number of "characters" in your name (i.e. my last name is Chester, but in *katakana* it's che-su-ta-a, with the long "a" counting as two characters). Note: With help from a teacher, Japanese friend, or even the *hanko*-maker, it may be possible to "translate" your name into *kanji* and have those characters carved into your *hanko*.

BASEMENTS

If you value your life, think twice about patronizing basement restaurants or bars. There are many of these establishments in Tokyo. At first you won't think anything about it. "I'm hungry; I'm thirsty," you'll say, and in you wander. Fine. Look around; do you see any exit signs except by the narrow staircase that you just walked down? No, you don't. What does that mean in an earthquake-prone country? Think about it. (See this chapter: "Safety Concerns.")

BICYCLES (also see Motorbikes)

Buying a *jitensha* (bicycle) in Tokyo is not a bad idea as you can use it to get to the station more quickly, as well as tote a bag of groceries home a little more easily (most bikes have baskets for that purpose). However, that's where the fun ends.

There seems to be a multitude of bicycle riders in Tokyo who are completely oblivious to the human beings around them. These bikers smoke, talk on phones and drink coffee as they careen down sidewalks with no concern for anyone else in the world. If they notice you for the split-second they may happen to look up from their leisure activities, they *may* ring their little bike bells, assuming you'll immediately jump out of the way—which you will, unless you want to be run over.

Also, except for major hub stations, you will often find bicycles parked in a haphazard way near subway/train stations. There does not seem to be any understanding that these bikes are blocking pedestrian paths. The Japanese seem to accept it. You, on the other hand, may go crazy stepping over or around bicycles just to get into the subway/train entrance. Do what I do: move the damn things out of the way!

Note: Japanese police have a penchant for stopping foreign cyclists for any reason they see fit and demanding to see identification, as well as proof of (bicycle) ownership. Carry these items with you at all times to avoid any cultural "misunderstandings." Also, if you park in an area deemed illegal (there are signs, but most are in Japanese, and even some of the Japanese have trouble understanding them) or park and forget about your bicycle for any length of time, you may return to find your bike has been removed. Yes, there are actually "bike removers" roaming around Tokyo's subway and train stations, checking to see that everyone's bike is properly parked (but, again, from the haphazard way that people park their bikes, it's a wonder all of them aren't removed for being public eyesores). If your bicycle is one of the unlucky ones, you will be able to reclaim it from a bike impoundment lot. But don't wait; after a month, bikes are auctioned off. Don't be one of those poor souls who ends up buying his/her own bike back!

CASH

In general, Japan is a cash-and-carry society. It's not that credit cards aren't accepted (they are), it's just that cash is preferred. In local shops that do not cater to foreigners, you may be stared at if you offer your credit card. At first this may irritate you, but if you go "cash-only" you might enjoy the thrill of buying only those things you actually have money for. Personally, I've found it strangely liberating. Cash paid, product in hand, no nasty bill collectors at my door, smile on my face.

Also: While it is true that there are thousands of convenience stores in Tokyo with ATMs, and while it is true that most people in Tokyo use either rechargeable prepaid IC cards for transportation and small purchases, it is still a wise idea to always have a ¥10,000 note tucked away in a billfold or purse. You'll thank me on those nights when you forgot to charge your IC card or can't find an ATM in the middle of the night and need the cash to take a taxi home.

CHEERFULNESS

It is essential to be cheerful in Tokyo. In fact, cheerful is the exact word used in many English-language classified ads. The Japanese are not people who complain or wear their hearts on their sleeves—and they expect you to follow suit. Being cheerful not only has great value in Japan, it's more beneficial than staring at walls and crying your eyes out because everything isn't right in your little world. So, cheer up; it's good for you.

CHIKAN

A *chikan* is a Japanese word used to describe a person (usually male) who thinks subways/trains are his personal sexual playground. In other words, someone who takes advantage of crowded conditions on public transportation to grope another individual who is trapped against his/her will (yes, gents, you might get "felt up," too). In the past, many Japanese women endured *chikan*, but in the last several years they have become much more vocal about this problem and there are now signs warning people about *chikan*; in addition, there are "women-only" passenger cars on some subway / train lines.

Since *gaijin* are easy targets, even if you are Mr. / Ms. Goody Two-Shoes, it is possible someone could "misunderstand" you repositioning yourself as a personal attack. Advice: Keep your wits about you, keep both hands where they can be seen and/or schedule your transportation to avoid rush hour. Easier said than done, I know.

CHRISTMAS/HOLIDAY SEASON

If Christmas (or whatever holiday you celebrate) is important to you, be aware that Christmas Eve in Japan is the year's biggest "date night," not "family and friend" time. Also, while the Japanese are great at putting up decorations and trees and flooding the world with Western Christmas songs, the "celebration" ends abruptly after December 25. In other words: no lingering warm feelings, colored lights, etc. But don't despair; create your own holiday season experience by being the loving *gaijin* who opens your *manshon* on Christmas Eve / Day to fellow homesick foreigners. It's amazing how strangers can quickly become friends under such circumstances.

CHRISTMAS CAKES

Every year about a week or two before December 25, you will notice Christmas cakes being sold in Tokyo by every bakery, coffee shop, casual dining establishment and anyone else who can figure out how to sell them. For their size (miniscule), these cakes are monstrously overpriced (anywhere from US$25-50), so if having a festive cake during the holidays is important to you, consider making it yourself.

Also: If you are anywhere within the vicinity of an establishment that sells Christmas cakes, and it is getting closer to (or actually is) Christmas day, be prepared for a sort of mass hysteria that includes shop employees with lungs of steel standing in front of little displays filled with little cakes, endlessly shouting and screaming as loud as possible that Christmas cakes are for sale.

If you wait till the day after Christmas, the prices go down, but, as everyone knows, what good is a Christmas cake the day after Christmas?

COFFEE (👂 "Coffee Shops")

Coffee was never the drink of choice in Japan, but, in a way, it could be said it is now, certainly in Tokyo. Almost everywhere you look there is not only a Starbucks or a Starbucks-wannabe, but also vending machines that sell endless varieties of canned coffee. So, it must follow that "bottomless cups" of coffee are the norm in Japanese restaurants, right? Wrong. While you can find the elusive bottomless cup at coffee shops like Denny's and Anna Miller's (chain coffee shops scattered throughout Tokyo; 👂 "Coffee Shops"), if you make the mistake of asking for more coffee almost anyplace else, you'll get it—and pay for it, dearly. This will hurt badly if you order a cup of java at a nice hotel where you will pay upwards of ¥1,000 so you can have the pleasure of drinking from a pretty china cup. Ask before you order that second cup o' joe!

CONVENIENCE STORES (*konbini*)

There are thousands of *konbini* in Tokyo, sometimes directly across the street from each other: 7-11, Lawson's, Family Mart and others not as well known. In addition to junk food and nukeable junk food, some carry limited fresh produce and alcoholic beverages. Whatever the item, rest assured it is two to three times as expensive as it would be at your regular supermarket (except canned coffee, soft drinks, etc., which are or should be priced exactly as they are in the vending machines lined up directly in front of the *konbini*).

Most *konbini* come equipped with copy machines, and some carry *The Japan Times* newspaper (which, though not the treasure trove of classified ads it once was, still carries a fair number of choice jobs in its Monday edition).

Generally speaking, *konbini* are open 24/7, so, yes, they *are* convenient. But they all have fluorescent lights bright enough to blind you and in the summer months, with lights a-blazin' and air conditioners a-blastin', they are a major drain on the city's electric supply. This is important only in the respect that every year there is a discussion about how *konbini* should conserve energy during the summer months and every year nothing changes. Draw your own conclusions.

COMPLAINING

There are times when you will complain about life in Tokyo. This is natural for many Westerners (including yours truly). However, if you have Japanese colleagues and/or are in a relationship with a Japanese, do not expect them to side with you. They may sympathize, but they will most likely offer an alternative (and sometimes culturally surprising) view of whatever situation you feel the need to complain about. They may also suggest you *gaman* (persevere) until you get past your problem. This is something they are taught from childhood: *gaman suru* (persevere under difficult circumstances) and *gambaru* (fight on, never give up). More likely than not your Japanese colleague/mate will tell you to "*Gambatte!*" ("Give 'em hell!" "You can do it!") when the going gets tough; you, in turn, will soon find yourself doing the same.

If you do decide to complain, present your complaint as if to say something has happened that you can't quite understand. This gentle approach will gain you a sympathetic ear.

CONCERTS AND EVENTS ($)

All major recording artists, international art exhibits, ballets, operas and more eventually come to Tokyo. Ticket prices for these events are prohibitively high, so be prepared to shell out. Also, prices for matinees, weekdays and weekends are often exactly the same, offering no incentive or advantage for attending one performance over another.

COUNTER-CULTURE SHOCK

You are going to experience this if you stay in Japan for any period of time, and it's good to experience it. It wakes up your mind and makes you think about who you are, who you've been and who you might become.

When you return to your own country, simple things like tipping waitstaff and taxi people will give you pause. After all, now you're used to getting waited on and driven around without having to give anyone extra. Or perhaps in the middle of winter you'll remember how nice it was to go to that *onsen* (hot spring) where the bubbly hot waters rejuvenated you (and how comfortable you've become being nude in front of others). But probably the thing that will shock you the most and have you back on the next plane to Japan: the sad state of salaries for skilled workers. Fact: even now, long after Japan's bubble economy has collapsed, you can make more as an English teacher in Tokyo than you can for any number of jobs in Western countries which require skills, knowledge, degrees, certificates or more. So when you start thinking: "I've had enough of Japan; I'm going home"—think carefully. Before you go back, check *craigslist.com* (an all-purpose classified ads site). You'll see salaries that have been frozen in time for the last twenty years. (They've been frozen in time in Japan, as well, but they've *always* been higher!) You'll turn off your computer, look at the walls of your tiny Tokyo apartment and think: "I could fix this place up."

There are harsh realities to face when you return home. As many challenges as you face in Japan, remember—it might seem better back home, but once you've seen both sides of the coin you will likely discover that unless you can have the best of both worlds (which is possible with tremendous effort), you'll never really feel the way you did before coming to Japan.

CRIME

It is often publicized that Japan has a low-crime rate. That does not translate into "Japan is crime-free." Within popular areas like Roppongi, Shinjuku, Shibuya and Ikebukuro, there are numerous clubs, hostess bars, massage parlors and more that often cater to a foreign clientele. There are often reports of spiked drinks, stolen credit cards and other unfortunate experiences that befall the naïve foreigner who thinks they are going to have an "adventure." You might—but not necessarily the one you hoped for. Keep your wits about you.

However, despite the existence of crime—foreign or domestic—as an American, in my experience, Tokyo is still safer than many major American cities. For example, I have walked back to my Tokyo apartment in the dead of night, carrying my wallet casually in my hand, without ever being assaulted or pickpocketed. (That's *not* to say it hasn't happened to others.) I have also left bags, books and valuables in Tokyo offices, coffee shops and restaurants (not to mention dropping my own alien registration card somewhere in Narita Airport!) and I have recovered every item either by returning to the place I left it and/or by having it returned to me by some kind Japanese person who went out of their way to track me down. All of this has contributed to a feeling of safety that I never once felt when I lived in Los Angeles or New York.

That said, if you do decide to venture into some of the shadier parts of town, bring a friend or colleague along with you and know where the nearest *kōban* (neighborhood police station) is.

CROWS

Everyone knows crows rule Tokyo. These black beasts are clever and completely unafraid of human beings. It also doesn't help that the Japanese put their garbage in clear plastic bags on the street three times a week. Crow sees bag; crow tears bag open; crow drags food remnants, unpaid bills and other scraps of a person's private life all over the street. This cycle never ends because after the crow has gotten its goodies, the aftermath is cleaned up by the neighborhood *ojīsan* (grandfather) or *obāsan* (grandmother), broom and dustpan at the ready, making the street presentable again.

DIRTY STRAW SYNDROME

Considering how obsessed the Japanese are with cleanliness (check out subway stations and see how spotless they are), and considering most restaurants give customers an *oshibori* (a moistened towelette, sometimes hot, sometimes cold) before they start their meal, it is incomprehensible how they are willing to let waitstaff jab a plastic straw into their soft drinks—jab it in with hands that have either been collecting money or lipstick-smudged/snot-filled napkins from people's tables. My favorite place was a "fresh juice bar" where the woman behind the counter took my order, threw the fruit into a blender, poured it, took my money, stuffed it into the cash register, *then* picked up a straw with the same hand that had just taken my money and jabbed a straw into my drink. Suddenly I wasn't thirsty.

This isn't always the case; there are places that have straws in paper wrappers. Just be aware of this situation if you don't like your drinks contaminated with someone else's hand germs.

DRIVING (§ "Driver's License")

There are any number of foreigners in Tokyo who drive cars (and motorbikes). I am not one and cannot see the point of being one since there is punctual public transportation and a fleet of taxis on call 24/7. However, if you *must* have your own set o' wheels and don't mind driving down lanes that haven't been widened since Tokyo was still called Edo, paying for highly-taxed gasoline and tolls every time you blink, paying annual "maintenance fees" to put your vehicle through a battery of tests (even when it's still relatively new), and paying exorbitant prices to park twenty minutes away from where you live (because most *manshon* buildings do not have an underground garage), you will need to get an International Driver's License. There is a mass of info available online and I've put some links on the *FIT* site. Good luck.

EARTHQUAKES (§ "Earthquakes")

If you have issues with earthquakes (*jishin*) you may not want to live in Tokyo for an extended period. Earthquakes occur often, and the most recent one (2011) was so devastating on so many levels that many foreigners quickly left, never to return (they were referred to as "fly-jins," a play on the word *gaijin*). If you choose to live here, you must accept that earthquakes come with the territory, so to speak. Plan accordingly. (Also, see this section, "Basements.")

ELEVATOR GIRLS

If you're lucky, you might still catch a glimpse of the "elevator girls," a fast-disappearing breed of service personnel in certain major department stores. If you do see them, please do not be rude or bother them with stupid questions or requests for photographs. Try to imagine standing all day inside what amounts to a closet, your face pressed into a plate of brass buttons, robotically repeating super-polite phrases, all while wearing a powder-puff pink suit with matching pumps and a pillbox hat.

ENGLISH "ACCENTS"

There are certain native English speakers who believe they not only have to dumb down their English to be understood by the Japanese, but that they must speak it in a mash of accents that can only be described as "drunk alien" (alien as in from outer space). Words are slurred, vowels are broadened, all "c" and "s" sounds are automatically pronounced as "sh," and faces become bizarre masks resembling stoned Kabuki actors.

Those Japanese who have taken the time to study English want you to speak ENGLISH; not "alienese." Please, do not insult anybody by modifying your pronunciation to the point of making it incomprehensible.

ENTRANCES/EXITS

See SAFETY CONCERNS.

FAX MACHINES

While it is true we live in an e-mail/text-messaging world, fax machines still have value in Tokyo's business world. So when you purchase your first "Tokyo landline phone," make sure it's a phone/fax/answering machine. A phone/fax was my first "investment" in Japan and it has repaid me many times over—so will yours.

FELLOW FOREIGNERS

There was a magical time in Tokyo years ago where you would see a fellow foreigner on the street, smile and say "hello." You might have even ended up becoming friends. This willingness to smile and greet strangers has sadly disappeared from modern-day Tokyo. If the opportunity presents itself, I encourage you to greet a fellow foreigner, even if it's just with a nod of the head. In this way I must say the Japanese, though they often shun foreigners, sometimes make attempts to be more friendly than any number of Westerners who pass each other with a sort of "I see you might be an English-speaking person, but I'm not interested in acknowledging that" look. It's your choice, but I opt for saying "hello."

FIRE HAZARDS

See SAFETY CONCERNS.

FOOD

Curry

Curry is served everywhere in Japan. However, there is a distinct difference between the aromatic curry from India served with *nan* and saffron rice, and what the Japanese call curry (or *karē*): an extremely mild, gluey brown sauce with chunks o' somethin', served with Japanese rice. This type of curry is found on almost every coffee shop menu in Japan. If, however, you want Indian or Thai curry, you're in luck as Tokyo boasts a sea of Indian and Thai restaurants. The Japanese love these curries, too, but when push comes to shove, they choose their own. So, think twice before you order curry at any restaurant other than one that serves legitimate Indian or Thai cuisine.

Ham (👂 "Coffee Shops/Restaurants")

For some reason, ham is worshipped in Japan. I'd say it is second to rice as the ingredient most often appearing in anything. "Quality" ham can only be found safely out of your reach behind glass-encased displays at pricey department stores. Otherwise, you will most likely come face-to-face with what I like to call "pink substances," mainly at coffee shops that include "food" on their menus. As a freelancer you will spend lots of downtime in Starbucks, its carbon copy Excelsior or its poorer cousins, Doutor and Pronto. As all are trying to promote a "coffee culture," food is limited to questionable sandwiches and salads. For some reason these items are always filled with some kind of smoked, raw, pressed or otherwise "prepared" ham. If there are six selections to choose from, four will have ham. The other fun thing about ham is that ham shows up in tiny bits and pieces in salads, gratin dishes, soups—you name it. If you are a vegetarian, confirm with the waitstaff that there is no ham in your order. I have gone out with any number of vegan friends who are deeply disturbed to find there is either ham in their order or that it has been cooked in a ham-flavored broth. You've been warned.

It's not on the menu (👂 "Eating at a Restaurant")

Don't waste time deciding what you want at a Japanese restaurant. I can almost guarantee as soon as you place your order you will be informed it's no longer available. This can be within the first 10 minutes a restaurant is open. Always ask first what *isn't* available. This will send the waitstaff scurrying to the kitchen, then back to you with the information you should have had in the first place. *Now* you can order.

O-zōni

This is a hot soup that is an essential part of *o-sechi-ryori* (Japanese New Year's cuisine). In addition to vegetables, chicken or fish, the soup contains large blocks of *mochi* (sticky rice pounded into a cake, then steamed). I mention this soup because every year a certain number of Japanese senior citizens *die* because they choke to death on *mochi*. The *mochi* in the *o-zōni* tends to be extremely thick and gluey, making it a challenge to eat. Count on seeing some horrific report about how an elderly Japanese person "enjoyed" *o-zōni* with family members—only to die a few hours later.

If you end up staying in Japan for any length of time, you too will get a chance to eat this soup—and see how easily someone could choke on it. Take small bites of the *mochi*, chew long and carefully, then swallow. Don't expect to carry on a conversation while doing this. If anybody tries to engage you in one, be suspicious. *Bon appetit!*

Overpriced meals, small portions, restricted quantities

Except for a few cheap restaurants (which invariably serve noodle dishes or brown curry), food in Japan is overpriced and portions are small. This goes for both restaurants and supermarkets.

At many supermarkets ("super" is not the word that will come to mind when you visit one) you will find most fruits and vegetables have been pre-selected, pre-weighed and placed in plastic bags; you will rarely have the opportunity to choose your own. Also, certain fruits and vegetables, including apples, grapefruits and cucumbers, are priced per piece.

You can also buy food in major department stores (always located on B1 and B2 basement floors), but prices there are two-to-three times higher than at your local supermarket. At these department stores, you will also encounter the Japanese custom of wrapping individual pieces of fruit as if they were Fabergé eggs. This seems to require *tons* of Styrofoam netting and plastic.

You do have some alternatives: If your apartment has a balcony (most do), start planting herbs, cherry tomato plants and anything else you can, just to have something to throw in a salad without having to drain your bank account to buy the same things at a store.

To find *gaijin*-sized portions in restaurants, read the restaurant reviews on any English-language social media sites or apps. As for what a Westerner would consider a normal-sized container of food or milk or chips or ice cream, you might have some luck at supermarkets that cater to Westerners (§ "Food").

Set courses/No substitutions

Many restaurants in Japan offer "set courses." This means set; all decisions have been made. The concept of substitution is completely foreign in Japanese restaurants, so if you're a picky eater, stick to restaurants that cater mainly to Westerners.

What do you think about Japanese food?/Can you eat Japanese food?

For some reason, the Japanese do not seem to understand that there are many fans of Japanese cuisine throughout the world. They always appear amazed that foreigners can eat Japanese food and then become intent on grilling them to find out what their opinion is. Be prepared to be interviewed.

GARBAGE (§ "Garbage")

The Japanese have, unlike other unnamed countries, realized if they don't separate their *gomi* (garbage) into *moeru gomi* (burnable) and *moenai gomi* (non-burnable), they are going to be in trouble—or, perhaps, already are. For example, in my own *manshon*, we have two containers in the kitchen, one for plastic, one for burnable and two on the balcony, one for bottles and cans, the other for PET bottles and Styrofoam trays (all which are supposed to be cleansed, sorted and brought to recycling centers) and two containers for paper (one for newspaper, the other for other kinds of papers, with staples, etc. removed).

What does all this mean? Learn to live with your garbage—a challenge in a small space. Help promote a recycling consciousness by bringing your *own* bag when you shop. It is absolutely not necessary to introduce more plastic bags into the environment, so do your part. (Also see this chapter: "Plastic.")

Note: Make sure you know what kind of garbage to put out on what day. (There are usually bilingual signs posted near residential buildings indicating such.) If you are unsure, ask your landlord, neighbor or call your *kuyakusho*. If you don't properly separate your *moeru gomi* and *moenai gomi*, do not be surprised to find that same *gomi* piled in front of your door. Yes, someone is making sure the *gaijin* is doing his/her civic duty and handling *gomi* in the proper way. *Don't* underestimate this chore!

Last, check public calendars posted near your building, especially at the end of the year. Japan essentially shuts down over the holidays immediately preceding and following January 1. If you don't dump your *gomi* in time for the year's last pick-up, be prepared to store it until regular pick-ups resume.

GAY/LESBIAN (§ "Gay / Lesbian")

The LGBT community in Tokyo is slowly making its voice heard, albeit not as loudly as it has been heard in the West. As of this writing, two of Tokyo's 23 wards now offer same-sex partners a certificate indicating the status of their relationship. It is not yet a marriage certificate, but it is a step towards recognition. Also, there are several gay or lesbian politicians who have been elected in recent years, so progress is being made.

Meanwhile, pressure from family and colleagues for Japanese men and women to marry at an "appropriate age" is still extremely high. This results in many married Japanese men, in particular, having a "gay lifestyle" on the side. Japanese lesbians, married (to men) or single, seem to be much quieter about their choices.

If you are a member of the LGBT community and decide to have a relationship in Japan with a Japanese national, be aware that you might face certain hardships as you get older (i.e. the possibility of being separated from the one you love due to visa issues) unless you either obtain permanent residency in Japan or have the right to marry your Japanese same-sex partner in your own country. Things will change in this regard, too, in Japan, but most certainly at glacial speed (and I'm talking pre-global warming glacial speed).

GIFTS

On occasion you may receive fresh fruit or a small cake from a student or colleague for having done what you thought was your job. The first time this happened I didn't know how to respond. The second time I offered a gift in return. I learned this wasn't necessary and that the gift did not necessarily have any hidden meaning. I received these gifts mostly from private students. After a while I found it a lovely gesture and simply thanked them. Eventually those gifts made me realize that if I was only thinking about the ¥5,000 I was going to get at the end of the hour, I needed an attitude adjustment. I became grateful for the gifts and hoped I lived up to whatever it was the student or colleague thought of me.

GOLDEN WEEK

Golden Week is a series of holidays starting April 29 that fall close enough together to sometimes equal about a week or more (with weekends). During this time many businesses close and people rush to get out of town to spend a few precious days having fun. However, if you join this crowd you will discover that the cost for most transportation to get you out of town has doubled or tripled. Best bet: stay in Tokyo, which will actually be quite peaceful and stress-free. In fact, there's nothing nicer than to casually stroll into a subway car, pick out the seat of your choice, sit back and read a novel (or a copy of *FIT*), and enjoy the unique feeling of being almost entirely alone in a major metropolis, knowing everyone else is struggling to get a patch of beach in Thailand or fighting to share a wave in Hawaii.

GUIDE PEOPLE

It is hard to describe the feeling that comes over you when you are late for an appointment because you are standing in the middle of Tokyo, lost, clueless, paralyzed with fear. Yes, you have a map; no, you don't understand it. Yes, you have an address; no, you can't read it. In a panic you rush to the first Japanese person you see and pray they can help. What may happen, to your amazement, is that they will stop whatever they are doing and walk with you *all the way to your destination*! The first time this happened to me I was dumbfounded. Not every Japanese person will respond this way, which will ultimately lead you to a *kōban* where you will also receive assistance with directions, but only verbal (almost always in Japanese, and, sorry to say, not always correct). If you do encounter the "Guide People" as you stumble through Tokyo's nooks and crannies, thank them profusely—and promise me once you are comfortable in your new world that if you see a lost and confused foreigner turning a map like a pinwheel, stop and offer assistance. Maybe one day we'll all get to where we're going.

HEALTH INSURANCE (§ "Health Insurance")

There are two insurance programs available in Japan: national health insurance (*kokumin kenkō hoken*), which pays 70% of your medical bills as of this writing, and employee health insurance (*kaisha kenkō hoken*), which pays 80% of your medical bills, as of this writing. As a freelancer, it is unlikely you will be able to apply for employee health insurance—unless your visa sponsor is willing to add you to his/her group policy, which is always a possibility.

This leaves you with national health insurance as your option. The problem for those who pay out of their own pockets for the national health insurance program is: your premium is determined by how much money you earn. This can translate into premiums as high as ¥600,000+ a year. Also, once you enroll in the program, you can never leave it unless you leave Japan. (Well... you can leave the program—but funds from your bank account may also be seized to cover any period of time that you have not paid for. Also, note: No matter what your stance on paying national health insurance premiums, do *not* forget to pay your *jūminzei*, or local prefectural tax.)

There are many debates about the pros and cons of the Japanese health insurance system. I can say this much about it: If you don't make a lot of money, Japanese health insurance can be extremely affordable; if you do make a lot of money, it can be extremely expensive. Regardless, the care you receive will be exactly the same.

Whether you decide to join or not is up to you, but after many years of struggling with this choice, I am now extremely glad I have it.

As for the actual cost of a doctor visit in Japan: In my experience, visits ranging from treatments for colds to sore throat to pink eye have run anywhere from approximately ¥1,500-5000.

Whatever you do, *make sure* you have: 1) some kind of insurance that covers you in Japan/worldwide; 2) a widely accepted credit card; and 3) some emergency cash in case of God-forbid situations. Also, make sure you check "Resources" at the end of this book and/or the *FIT* website for a list of medical facilities where English is spoken. (Note: Medical facilities catering to the foreign community often will not accept national health insurance, only cash for payment—but at least you should be able to communicate with the doctor in English.)

HONORIFICS (§ "Honorifics")

Do not underestimate the value of honorifics (prefixes/suffixes used to beautify Japanese words or convey respect) when you speak Japanese. When the Japanese refer to you as "John-*san*/Mary-*san*," (or -*sama*, in super polite situations) it is not some quaint custom from days gone by.

Some honorifics are "built in" to certain nouns (*o-cha*, tea; *go-annai*, information, *o-kyaku-sama*, customer), and are almost always used for family members (*o-tōsan*, father; *o-kāsan*, mother). Your main concern is to make sure you use -*san* when you address people you are not on intimate or friendly terms with (and even sometimes with people you *are* on friendly terms with).

INSECTS

Dani (ticks)

These microscopic bloodsucking bastards embed themselves in your *tatami* mats, furniture and bedclothes. During the summer months you will often awaken to discover these mischievous monsters have polka-dotted your legs with bright red love bites, eliminating the possibility of wearing a nice pair of shorts on unendurably hot days. If you don't believe me, check out those who dare to bare their legs when the heat hits.

The Japanese don't really seem to have an issue with *dani*; they just endure it as part of getting through the summer. You, on the other hand, may not feel the same (literally). To deal with the "aftermath" of both *dani* and *ka* (mosquitoes; see below), your local drugstore will have gels, creams, salves and more, prominently displayed during the "biting season" to help you find some (temporary) relief.

Ka (mosquitoes)

Mosquitoes in Japan seem to be thirstier and crueler than their Western cousins. If you like to show off your legs in summertime and are dumb enough to go anywhere near a pond or lake, be prepared to come back with welts the size of golf balls on your calves.

Semi (cicada)

There are many who are enchanted by the unique sounds that the cicada creates with its timbals. If you are among them, you will enjoy its buzzy summer symphony. If you are not, pack your earplugs, because you will not be able to escape these merry noisemakers during the summer season.

JAPANESE HOLIDAYS (§ "Japanese Holidays")

If you do not already have a Japanese calendar, get one. The reason: You may want to make a reservation to go out of town—without realizing 12 million other people want to do the same thing because it's a holiday weekend. Also, you may happily go to visit a park, museum or any other attraction you think would be open to the public, but isn't—because it's a holiday. (What is the logic of closing a public place on a day people could actually *enjoy* it? Good question.)

JAPANESE LANGUAGE STUDY (§ "Japanese Language Study")

By all means study Japanese, whether at one of Tokyo's multiple language institutes or by finding a language exchange partner via social media. Both offer great networking opportunities as well: I found my first music job through a fellow language student, which led to many other jobs and years of income.

It is absolutely to your advantage to take the Japanese Language Proficiency Test (JLPT), which, as of this writing, is held twice a year in Japan and other countries around the world. There are four levels (1-5), with Level 5 being the easiest. I encourage you to at least pass Level 3, and preferably Level 2. By doing so, you are certain to find an entire other level of attractive jobs available for you in Tokyo.

For those of you who don't think it's important to study the language because you won't use it after you leave: The more you fight learning Japanese, the less successful you will be in Japan. Make the effort to be as proficient as possible and I promise it will pay off multifold.

JAPLISH/ENGRISH (§ "Japlish/Engrish")

Whatever you want to call it, the mixing of these two languages creates special words that bring levity to life. Many of these creations are, inexplicably, applied to chocolates, cookies or crackers. Here are a few choice examples of real product names:

> "Air Smash"; "Angel Sweet Asse"; "Beer Choco"; "Crack Up"; "Crum"; "Collon"; "Crunky"; "Pecker"; and the hands-down winner: "Titlis."

If you wrinkle your nose in disgust upon seeing product names with English-language word combos that sound like they were dreamt up after ingesting heavy drugs, you may want to consider finding a nice job shelving ancient grammar tomes at a library in a little seaside village far away from everybody and everything. For the rest of you who enjoy having your sense of reality tampered with, welcome to Japan!

KAWAII

Translated as "cute," "darling," or "adorable," *kawaii* is the war cry of all Japanese teenage girls (and some Japanese women, as well). If a girl or boy is lucky enough to be considered *kawaii,* she/he is set for life. Being *kawaii* is much more important than being beautiful or intelligent; it is a key to all the universe has to offer. Those amongst us who are not *kawaii* can only stand on life's sidelines, wiping tears away as we watch an endless parade of *kawaii* people, accompanied by Hello, Kitty® goods, anime creatures, *cosplay* ("costume play") characters and irritating little mascots. The great thing is, though, even if we can never be part of the *kawaii* kingdom, we are encouraged, in Japanese movies, TV shows, CMs and anywhere an advertisement can be placed, to buy everything *in* the *kawaii* kingdom. In this way we can still have the happiness that would have otherwise eluded us forever.

KITCHENS

Next to the Japanese toilet room, the kitchen is the smallest room you will find in your *manshon/apāto*. Why this is escapes me since I would say a good 60% of Japanese television shows are dedicated to cooking—something you can't do in your *own* kitchen unless you have the elasticity of a cartoon character and/or are constantly able to suck in your gut and walk sideways. If you are used to living in big city apartments with tiny kitchens, you won't have issues. If not, don't hang your steak knives on the kitchen wall! (See this chapter: "Space.")

LAUNDRY

Some Japanese apartments have a space specifically designed for a stackable washing machine (with a hook-up for cold water only) and dryer. Alternatively, people will put their washing machines on their "verandas" (mini-balconies) if space allows. If either space is available to you, get your own washer/dryer. If not, you will find yourself trudging through the snow at 6:00 a.m. on winter mornings to use one of the two machines at your local *koin randorī* (Laundromat).

Note: If you must use the *koin randorī*, be aware that some people enjoy smoking as they do their laundry. The fact that you used a fabric softener to bring some "spring freshness" to your clothes will be lost on them. Since the early bird gets the machine and usually avoids the smoking contingent, set those alarm clocks at the crack o' dawn and spend the day in clean clothes!

LOVE HOTELS (§ "Love Hotels")

A "love hotel" (known elsewhere as a "no-tell motel") is where you and your partner can shag yourselves into a stupor without bothering your neighbors or, more likely, your wife or husband. In brief, you pay a set amount for a "rest period" (*kyūkei*) and then… you know! But all love hotels are not created equal, so make sure you first check the § on the *FIT* website.

MAKE-UP MAVENS, ETC.

Over the last several years it has become popular in Tokyo for young women to apply their make-up while they are on the subway/train. This may not bother some; I don't belong to that group. I personally do not appreciate someone who has decided to turn the entire carriage into her personal toilette. This type of girl, who I like to call a PYM (Pretty Young Miss), will take out her entire arsenal of cosmetics and very, *very* slowly "do" her face. While this might be great training for people who want to study how other people put on their make-up, for the rest of us who have to endure endless eyelash stroking, split-end trimming, mascara, blush and lip gloss application, it is extremely unpleasant. So, I figure, if a woman can put on her make-up, a man can certainly shave his beard and clip his nose hairs. What's the difference?

In tandem with PYMs, you will also find the Facestuffers (who chow down on their "aromatic" meals, oblivious to the olfactory senses of others), the Drink Chuggers (who do their best to down big cans of beer before the next stop) and my personal favorite, the Exotic Pet Hiders (who surreptitiously cradle their frightened African bush babies inside their jackets).

So, for those that may feel that the subway/train is an enclosed space in which we must respect others, I'm sorry to report that, at least in Tokyo, it is a quaint concept of years gone by.

MANSHON

See APĀTO.

MASKS

You will often see people wearing surgical masks in Tokyo. Do not let this alarm you. It means they either have a cold, a respiratory ailment or they don't want to die by inhaling the next round of contagious air-borne viruses. You may laugh or joke about these masks, but at some point you may also be wearing one for the very reasons stated here.

MEDICAL MATTERS (§ "Clinics/Hospitals")

Doctors, hospitals, medicine and related matters are beyond the scope of this book. Check the "Resources" chapter of this book as well as the *FIT* website for links to English-speaking medical facilities and more.

However, there is one important piece of advice I can impart: If you go to see a Japanese physician or visit a clinic and you are given a prescription of any kind, make sure you ask for a *one-week supply*; if not, you will be given a three-day supply. Why? So you can come back again and pay to be "checked" and pay to get more medicine.

MISUNDERSTANDINGS

It goes without saying that when communicating with someone from another country there are bound to be misunderstandings. I only point this out because I have experienced some harsh moments in Japan because of my American humor. The Japanese sense of humor does not include the sarcastic, sitcom-esque humor so loved by Americans. When I've attempted to interject jokes into a conversation, even with Japanese people I have known for years, I have often encountered bewilderment, confusion and anger. On the other hand, if I've attempted more clownish or silly humor, I've been more successful at getting laughs. If you want any guidelines, turn on Japanese TV—you'll get the idea instantly.

MONEY

Money earned, saved or spent in Tokyo requires its own book, but for now a few thoughts: Almost everything in Tokyo is overpriced. As a result, money will flow out of you as if you were a sieve. On the other hand, you might have a lot more of it to play with/save. Tokyo can turn your life around financially (hence the reason for this book), but, as in any other big city, temptation is everywhere and you can lose large chunks of that yen by simply going to eat some *fugu* (blowfish) in Ginza.

As mentioned in "Save Your Money" (see "Jobs"), establish a financial goal and stick to it. While friends evaporate their salary on a hot night in Roppongi (where many of Tokyo's clubs and bars are located), you will have sent your money home and be watching the interest grow.

To again quote my friend Colleen Sakurai, "Big money comes easy; small money comes hard." If you don't know what that means yet, you will after living in Tokyo for a few years.

NARROW STREETS

In Tokyo there are many streets that are so narrow it is almost impossible for a car and a single person to pass through at the same time. As the Japanese have grown up with this situation, it doesn't seem odd to them to be constantly dodging motorbikes and cars. You, on the other hand, might have to stuff yourself into the doorframes of people's homes just so traffic can pass.

Advice: Under no circumstances walk through the streets wearing headphones. While there are polite drivers here, there are many others who drive as fast as they can, oblivious to anything (and anyone) that might be in their way. Consider yourself warned.

NEWS (Television)

Regardless of what the top stories of the day might be, Japanese TV news seems to eventually focus on Japan's sports stars, weather and Japanese people making, selling or eating Japanese food. If you enjoy these things, you will have a great time watching the news.

NHK (§ "Media")

NHK is *Nippon Hoso Kyokai*, or Japan Broadcasting Corporation. This is Japan's sole public broadcaster and it expects to receive fees (on the NHK website, look under "Receiving Fee System") so you can have the privilege of watching their riveting, thought-provoking programs in your own home. Whether you want to pay those fees is immaterial; NHK sends minions to collect them. However, don't hesitate to remind the minions that in 2004, 30,000 viewers refused to shell out because of a teensy "embezzlement scandal" involving millions of yen and an NHK staff producer. Unfortunately, that hasn't stopped NHK from trying to collect fees. So if you do break down and pay up, a little "NHK" marker will be prominently displayed near your front door so that the minions will stop bothering you.

NOISE

Note: While what I describe below is true, it is not true in every situation. So if noise doesn't bother you, you won't have any issues. If it does, carry earplugs with you—everywhere.

Background "Music" (BGM)

At many food and beverage establishments, background music ("BGM") is generally quite loud. However, you (being a foreigner) can politely ask for the BGM to be turned down. You'll need to have it turned down if you expect to be able to concentrate on anything. (§ "Coffee shops/Restaurants: Complaints")

Exercise classes

If you attend a sports club in Tokyo, whether to exercise with machines or to go swimming, and there happens to be an aerobics class taking place anywhere in the general vicinity (including the swimming pool), be aware that the aerobics music will be pushed up to deafening levels.

Public Announcements

If you happen to be doing freelance work from home, you will hear, at any given hour of the day, unbearably loud announcements blasting out of cheap loudspeakers attached to a cheap truck as it crawls down your road, advertising laundry poles, roasted sweet potatoes, flea markets, recycled goods or something else that requires your immediate attention. It will require immediate attention because it is so loud that short of puncturing your own eardrums, you won't be able to focus on anything else until they've passed by. There is no way to prepare for this except to have sturdy earplugs at the ready. Otherwise, I strongly suggest checking out one of the city's numerous shared office spaces. (§ "Shared Office Spaces")

Supermarket Announcements

If you are sensitive to sounds, you will have definite issues at most Japanese supermarkets (*sūpā*). The only things "super" about them are the loud sounds emanating from strategically placed boomboxes. As you wander down tiny aisles with your tiny shopping basket (forget carts), the bones in your inner ear will be vibrating so hard you'll think you're in the midst of an air raid. Management, realizing you are a captive audience, simultaneously bombards you from every vantage point with a variety of daily special announcements, all delivered rapidly, repeatedly and, of course, *loudly*. Accompanying the announcements is music that sounds like it was modeled on the marching songs of Chinese peasant women. In addition, synthesized versions of Japanese pop songs are played non-stop in the background (or what's left of it) to ensure that your shopping experience is indeed a pleasant one. Enjoy!

Train Announcements

I've included this under "Noise" because there is no other way to describe what amounts to loud shouting over loudspeakers. Before the subway/train arrives, you will hear a recorded announcement (sometimes with a female's voice on one side of the track, a male's voice on other side of the track) letting you know the next train is on its way, to stand behind the yellow (or white) line and to be careful.

In addition to these announcements, many subway/train stations now have their own cutesy "theme songs" played at deafening levels to alert you to the fact that the doors will be closing shortly. To add one more layer of "fun," some major subway stations have installed numerous flat panel displays where, while you wait for the next train, you are forced to watch and, more importantly, *listen* to an endless barrage of noisy ads and movie trailers.

When you are actually inside a subway/train, the conductor will be sure to let everyone know about the upcoming station, not to forget anything, the upcoming station, again, and a gracious thanks for having used that particular line. Problem: No one doing this job seems to have been taught how to properly use a microphone (or to enunciate). This results in announcements that are inaudible, garbled or so loud that you'll want to start running for cover (difficult inside a subway/train). Good luck!

PACHINKO PARLORS

If your idea of fun is a noisy, smoky gambling area where glazed-eyed creatures with cigarettes permanently attached to their mouths sit transfixed in front of pinball-like machines, watching as metal balls ping their way into oblivion, you'll have found your Nirvana.

PAPER/PAPER PRODUCTS

Napkins

In Japan, a country that prides itself on its multitude of paper products, it is often rare to find napkins in restaurants (or paper towels—or toilet paper—in restrooms). On the other hand, you will most certainly be offered an *oshibori* (the moist towelette mentioned earlier) before beginning your epicurean adventure. The hot ones are great because they're real towels; the cold ones are basically wet paper towelettes, wrapped in cheap, crinkly plastic.

To wipe the greasy broth that will certainly dribble down your chin as you slurp up hot *ramen*, pack an extra handkerchief. However, beware: In Japan, handkerchiefs are generally not for wiping your mouth or for handling *hanamizu* ("nose water"), but for delicately mopping your brow when it gets too hot.

Tissue Issues

You will often see young Japanese folks handing out tissue packages throughout Tokyo, usually near subway/train stations. The tissue packages are often covered with advertisements for contact lenses, sports clubs, karaoke bars, hostess clubs or some kind of "dating"/"massage" service. When you are offered these tissues, take them! If you have to use a public restroom where there is *no* toilet paper, you will be forced to spend an additional

¥100 to buy the same package of tissues (see below, "Toilet Paper")—just with a different advertisement.

The most important thing to remember about tissue packages and other forms of advertisements (such as pamphlets, brochures) that are handed out on the street is: they are targeted at certain groups. The advertiser may specifically want women, men and/or foreigners. Often times, though, they do *not* want foreigners. Even though you may truly need some tissues or actually want to go to the new karaoke club advertised on the tissue package, try your best not to get your dander in a dither when you are clearly passed over by the "tissue people."

Toilet Paper

Toilet paper in public restrooms is *not* always available. However, ¥100 vending machines which sell packs of tissues are usually placed near or at the entrances to public restrooms. Regardless, always carry a pack of tissues with you, just in case.

PLASTIC

Japan is awash in plastic; it will surely one day sink under the weight of all the plastic wrapping manufacturers insist on smothering their products with. As you will certainly read elsewhere, the Japanese like to wrap things three times, whether or not the original product is already wrapped. So, as mentioned in "Garbage," when you go shopping, bring your own bag with you. Toss it in your briefcase or purse; when you're ready to make your nightly purchases from your local *konbini* (convenience store), show it to the cashier and say: *Kore o tsukatte kudasai.* ("Use this please.")

It's worth noting that as of this writing a number of stores have started to charge customers for plastic bags. Good. But after reading this, you'll be ahead of the game and won't need to contribute to the destruction of the earth any more than necessary.

PORNOGRAPHY

If you are prudish about sex, Tokyo might be unsettling in ways you hadn't anticipated. You will quickly encounter pornography, whether it be graphic illustrations in *manga* (Japanese comic) magazines, or blatant advertisements on subways/trains featuring semi-nude girls. There are also several newspapers that regularly stick in photos of sex acts amidst articles on baseball and politics. You may also have the misfortune of encountering child pornography.

Do not assume these things do not disturb the average Japanese citizen or that they tacitly approve of them. Talk with your Japanese friends and hear what they have to say. There is a growing awareness of the pornography problem and it is addressed in the media more often than it used to be. (§ "Media")

POST OFFICE ("Post Office")

A visit to the *yūbinkyoku* (post office) in Japan can be daunting. The envelope you are mailing is sometimes stared at for an inordinately long time, after which you may be interrogated regarding the envelope's contents. Its size may also be measured—over and over. Japan generally loves tiny, narrow envelopes which are just big enough to slip in a single sheet of rice paper, refashioned as an origami Isosceles triangle. (Don't be surprised if you have to "repackage" your letter.)

As for English-language guidance: There are a few signs with English words at some post offices, but don't expect any. However, there is online information and phone assistance in English (§ "Postal Services"). To further help make your postal trip a pleasant one, see the section on "post offices" in "Helpful Phrases."

Peak times to avoid post offices are any gift-giving seasons (*ochūgen*, mid-summer gift, and *oseibo*, end-of-year gift) and any time near New Year's Day. Unlike Western countries that flood mailboxes with Christmas cards, the Japanese send out *nengajō* (New Year cards). If you go to the post office during these times, invariably there is only one postal employee with a line of 50 people to serve, while the rest of the staff "busy" themselves in the backroom. (I've always wondered what's going on back there, haven't you?)

PROPAGANDA TRUCKS (*gaisensha*)

This topic should be listed under "Noise," (see this chapter, "Noise") but I felt it required its own special mention.

There are certain people in Japan who still believe that foreigners should not be allowed in as they pollute the purity of Japan. Those people are known as the *uyoku* (right-wing nationalists). They drive around in *gaisensha* (huge black propaganda trucks often decorated with oversized *kanji* and images of the war flag of the Imperial Japanese Army). The truck's loudspeakers alternately spew ancient war songs and hate speech at ear-splitting levels. If they drive by or park near where you are working, or are ahead of you in traffic, you are stuck with the noise, since whatever regulations about noise levels in Tokyo are apparently not enforced. The only good thing is that, unless you are fluent in Japanese, you will not understand what they are saying (but you'll definitely *hear* it). (§ "Media")

PUBLIC RESTROOMS

While public restrooms in Japan are often miles ahead of those in other countries (i.e. many are generally clean, well-maintained, some with soap, some with hot air dryers), men in particular must be prepared to meet the "Toilet Lady." This poor soul, usually an *oba-san* in her late 50s/early 60s, has been entrusted with the task of wiping down the urinals, scraping off the porcelain and keeping the place tidy—while it's in use! Have pity on this person. It's a thankless job, but somebody's gotta do it, and, unlike other countries' restrooms where flies and vermin have settled in and established community centers, you'll secretly thank the Toilet Lady every time you use a public facility.

Drawbacks are psychological. What if you don't like "Mom" or "Auntie" hovering nearby as you tinkle? Tough. This gal (usually sturdy and stocky) is going to do her job one way or the other, so if you're pee-shy, get over it.

The only time you may encounter a problem is when you, bladder bursting, rush to a public restroom to encounter a signboard with the figure of a bowing maintenance man and a scribbled *kanji* message letting you know that Toilet Lady is busy doing something that requires you to use a different facility. You'll look around. There *is* no different facility. Play dumb; boldly ignore the sign and walk in. Do your business, leave. Toilet Lady might freak out, but most likely she'll ignore you. Don't worry about her; worry about your bladder. We are human beings, not machines.

RACISM

"Acceptable" foreigners in Tokyo's business world still tend to be attractive young Caucasians. People of African descent are almost always thought of as "entertainers," and people of other races fall into different categories depending on the shade of their skin or shape of their eyes. Also, sadly, there is still a tremendous amount of animosity between Japan and Korea, and Japan and China, based on World War II-related issues (which are still being reported on as I write these words!). Yes, we are now in the 21st century, but, to many people, certain things (Korean "comfort" women, the Nanking massacre, annual visits to Yasukuni shrine [§ "Yasukuni Shrine"] by Japan's prime minister, etc.) have never been properly addressed, and tempers flare at a moment's notice. In addition to hearing the *gaisensha* (see this chapter, "Propaganda Trucks"), if you live in Tokyo you will certainly find yourself reading about the planting of Japanese flags on islands that China or Korea or Russia also insist belong to them (§ "History"), lawsuits by surviving Chinese or Koreans who were forced to work for the Japanese in WWII and other disturbing stories.

These events are still covered in the news on almost a daily basis. The best thing that can be said is it will definitely open your eyes to a tragic period of history and perhaps affect you deeply enough to learn more about it.

REFRIGERATORS (*reizōko*)

Buy the absolutely biggest *reizōko* (refrigerator) you can fit into your kitchen (assuming you have one). You will thank me at the end of the day. Why? If you opt for a compact fridge, it will only hold enough food to feed a nest of wrens. Buy big, and live (and eat) like a human being.

RESTAURANTS (*resutoran*)

You can enjoy any type of cuisine you can imagine in Tokyo. Some ethnic restaurants adapt their dishes to suit the Japanese palate; others don't (or won't) bother. The latter is good, because you can taste the authentic cuisine and expand your culinary adventures.

Note: You may think it's fun to walk in, point at some squiggly *kanji* on a menu and take your chance with whatever shows up on the table. This is foolish because unless you can see the yen amount for each dish written clearly in Arabic numerals, you might end up paying family fortunes for tiny dishes of grilled eel (which may or may not be imported from China and passed off as "Japanese"). To avoid this make sure you ask if the restaurant has an English menu (some do, but only present it if you ask).

Certain small restaurants expect you to buy a ticket from a vending machine prior to getting your meal or actually give you the bill instantly after you order. You (sometimes) must pay first and hope for the best. This is *not* your usual scenario in Tokyo, so don't get upset if you encounter it.

One great thing: You don't have to worry about tipping at restaurants. On the other hand, some restaurants, depending on their size, location or feeling of importance, may include built-in "gratuities." For more on this, see this chapter: "Tips."

SAFETY CONCERNS

I have come to the conclusion there are no safety concerns in Tokyo—not until someone goes up in flames, plunges to their death at a train station or is crushed in a revolving door. I have personally been in theaters where people were sitting in aisles and blocking exit doors while a show featuring *flamethrowers* was in action! (If I had known, trust me, I wouldn't have been there.) I have walked down streets where an angel's wing was all that prevented oncoming cars from shaving off one of my arms. In addition, on a daily basis, I (and thousands of others) have had to stand so close to oncoming trains that the resulting *whoosh* of air has almost sucked us down onto the track. (Note: because of some unfortunate accidents and suicides, many stations now have sturdy barriers between platforms and tracks).

Oddly, I have never once heard a Japanese person complain about these situations—even if their own lives were endangered. There seems to be the attitude that it goes with the territory, deal with it. So, while I might not be able to take care of all of you, be aware you will encounter the following—and be prepared.

Entrances/Exits/Fire Hazards

Without fail, if there is a double-door at an entrance/exit to a building/shop, one will be locked (in fact, the "locked" door may have a permanent sign on it indicating it is not to be opened—even when there is only one entrance to a building!). I have seen it at the entrance of my own apartment building. As such I make it a habit to unlock the locked one. This is my way of letting Japan know that yes, there are emergencies, and some of us who may be trapped inside might want to get out of the building, preferably alive. For those people who will tell you that one door is locked because the "wind" might blow it open, the correct response is, "No, it *won't*."

Also, for small nightclubs, there is only ONE entrance/exit (see this chapter, "Basements"). This means that if you think going into a smoky "hostess club" or "snack bar" (on the fifth floor of a building wedged airtight between two other buildings) is going to be a fun, cultural experience, think hard. You will often find things (garbage, empty boxes, odds and ends) in the stairwells—things that might get in the way if you have to suddenly leave the premises in the event of an emergency. Also, some clubs apparently don't think it's important to ensure that their fire alarms are working. This can lead to tragedy, as it did in Kabuki-cho (an "entertainment" area in Tokyo) in 2001 where 44 people died because they couldn't get out of their tiny drinking hole when it was turned to ash in a blaze.

Last, and I think most importantly, major hotels in Tokyo also have hallways and stairwells littered with boxes, carts and God-knows-what, and, in my experience, they have almost always blocked fire extinguishers and exits. Because I worked as a musician at these hotels, I saw it for myself. I often would complain, sometimes nightly, until someone would "rearrange" things to shut me up—only to have things revert to how they were in a few days.

Do not buy into the fantasy that everything is safe and that no one can get hurt in Tokyo. You've been warned.

SHINKANSEN (§ "Travel")

You will think, "I'll take the *shinkansen* (lit. "new trunk line" or "bullet train" in English) and get out of Tokyo for the weekend. I'll relax and return with batteries recharged." You will be mistaken.

Once you're aboard, there will likely be frequent announcements. The majority of these will be to push ice cream, coffee, lunch boxes, ice cream, wine, and... I'm sorry, did I say ice cream? These interruptions are augmented by the constant sound of cheap plastic being ripped to shreds as fellow passengers dive into dried squid, *onigiri* (rice balls) and ice cream—although, miraculously, that won't be wrapped in plastic (but the plastic spoon that comes with it will be).

As for your view from the train window: There will be occasional patches of Japan's natural beauty, but unfortunately most of what you will see are endless building projects and slabs of concrete covering what once were lovely islands.

More importantly, perhaps, traveling via *shinkansen* is generally quite expensive. I can't tell you how many times I realized it was cheaper to fly to Los Angeles, spend a week at a decent hotel, enjoy great food at realistic prices and return to Japan—all for less than a round trip on the *shinkansen* for a three-night stay at a *ryokan* (Japanese inn) with an *onsen* (hot spring) in the Japanese countryside. Sad, but true.

(Note: If you are traveling at night, be aware that the train's bright fluorescent lights are not adjusted, so bring a sleep mask if you intend to get any rest.)

SHOPPING (*kaimono*)

It's very important to know that *kaimono* (shopping) is a way of life in Japan. For anybody who teaches English and asks what a student did over the weekend, the answer is often "shopping." As of this writing, the product-jammed Japanese website *rakuten.co.jp* still proudly proclaims: "Shopping is Entertainment!"

You may feel the same; if so, there are endless opportunities to spend your yen anywhere you go in Tokyo. To help find your heart's desire(s), I've included several links on the *FIT* website. However, I have one request, as mentioned earlier in this chapter: *Bring your own bag*. Some stores are starting to charge for plastic bags, so more folks are bringing their own "eco-bags." This is an encouraging indication that change is underfoot.

Other fun things to know: When you pay for something in Japan, your change is returned with your receipt. This may not be peculiar to Japan, but just be prepared. The receipt is laid across your hand, coins laid on top of the receipt. To me, it is very awkward to balance those coins on the receipt until you can safely transfer them to a wallet, coin purse or pocket. It's awkward because you must deal with it that instant or the cashier and customer behind you start staring you down.

Some people prefer receiving their receipts this way; for those that don't, this custom will quickly irritate. So, I've included phrases (👂 "Shopping") for this very situation to make clear to the staff to put the receipt <u>in</u> the bag. Thanks for letting me vent; I feel much better!

SHŪTEN (end of the line/final stop)

Some subway/train lines do not stop at every station and/or change their final stop depending on the time. Be aware of what the *shūten* is or you might end up having to exit somewhere you hadn't planned.

All stations have timetables indicating when the subway/train arrives and what stations will be stopped at. Also, on the station's digital signboards, as well as on the front of the train itself, the name of the *shūten* should be displayed clearly. If you have gotten on the wrong subway/train and you arrive at a certain station and everybody gets off, don't panic; most likely you have arrived at the *shūten*. Listen carefully for the announcements between stations; the *shūten* should be stated clearly and often. Also, some subways have a small display inside each car that indicates the final station with a blinking red light, making it clear whether you're headed for your destination (or not).

SMOKING (§ "Smoking Issues")

While there have been and continue to be efforts made to provide more non-smoking sections in the workplace and in public facilities, Japan is still a smoker's paradise.

Unfortunately, as long as there is a "cozy" relationship between the Japanese government's Ministry of Finance and the Japanese tobacco industry, smoking will continue to be an issue.

SNEEZING AND COUGHING

For some reason, there are certain people in this country (generally men, but not always), who feel sneezing and coughing without covering their mouths is their natural-born right. They feel this particularly when they are standing on an escalator in front of *you* while there is a strong current of air blowing in *your direction*.

This situation also occurs in crowded subways/trains where these same people don't realize that thousands of their virus-filled droplets have now just saturated *your* air space. More importantly, they don't understand why this would bother you.

Hence, this is another reason why some people wear surgical masks. (See this chapter: "Masks.")

SPACE

There isn't any. Inside your own home you will be bumping into things, knocking things off walls, pulling entire bookshelves down, getting your clothes caught on everything and eventually walking through your "area" as if it were filled with land mines.

A good way to confirm this reality is to see "model apartments." Go with a Japanese friend so the realtor will think you are a couple (they don't care if you are with a male or female, as long as one-half of your team is Japanese). The kitchens (see this chapter: "Kitchens") are rooms in name only. The only people qualified to prepare a meal in them are either acrobats from Cirque du Soleil or those blessed with eight limbs so they can stand in one spot and reach for anything they want without having to duck, twist or otherwise use pretzel logic. Bizarrely, both kitchens and washrooms have sinks large enough to bathe a newborn calf in—at the expense of counter space where, I don't know, maybe you'd want to slice up a nice apple.

If you like living, eating, sleeping, answering nature's call and "sexing" (Japlish for "having sex") inside itsy-bitsy compartments that would do Ken and Barbie proud, you'll be as happy as a mummy in a sarcophagus. If you're looking for *space*, take the next commercial flight to the moon.

SPEED LIMITS

Although I am sure they exist, I have never seen a posted speed limit in Tokyo, at least not in residential areas like mine, near schools where toddlers, weighted down with *randoseru* (backpacks) twice their size, brave their way down teensy lanes wide enough for a bunny to hop across. Oddly, these are the same lanes where bikers, pizza delivery boys and joy-riding speed freaks hurtle by at any given moment. The fact anyone's life may be in danger doesn't cross their minds (although it might cross yours).

This phenomenon can be seen even on the finest streets in town. It seems the purpose of most streets is just for cars to be able to drive from point A to point B; pedestrians are an afterthought.

The concept of speed bumps, which might actually prevent thousands of deaths or "accidental" amputations, seems to have escaped city planners.

SUPERMARKET STORE HOURS

There are few things more maddening in Tokyo then not being able to buy food at hours that are conducive to your schedule. Of course, you are free to go to the millions of *konbini* which sell great tummy-stuffers such as white flour buns filled with *anko* (see this chapter, "An"), or you can *gaman* (endure) and wait until 10:00 a.m. when your local *sūpā* has deigned to open. While this hour might have been appropriate when all men marched off to work and all women stayed behind doing breakfast dishes before heading down to buy enough food to fill their tiny refrigerators for one more day, it doesn't cut it in the modern world.

So, if you are used to doing your food shopping at all hours of the day or night, you are in for a shock. Despite being in a major metropolis serving a large population with varied working hours, Japanese supermarkets all seem to open at 10:00 a.m., with most of them closing at 8:00 p.m. (or 8:30 p.m. during the summer). Stock up while you can!

SWAB THOSE STEPS!

I know; one swabs decks, not steps. But remember, *this is Japan.*

At any given subway/train station you will encounter The Step People: cheerful senior citizens clad in brightly colored matching ensembles, happily scrubbing and hosing down the very steps you are trying to walk on. Watch as The Step People's soapy water splashes down the old stony pockmarked steps! Make a game of avoiding the rivulets that gravitate towards your feet, beckoning you to slip, fall and smash your head open to the amusement of bystanders who won't lift a finger to help! Revel in the challenge of getting to work—without getting killed!

Instead of scheduling these "cleaning sprees" at hours where a minimal number of people would be inconvenienced, the public transportation companies have decided you should see The Step People in action—clear reminders of what might happen to *you* if you don't save every yen you've ever earned and find yourself over 50, desperate and hungry. As with the Toilet Lady, don't get angry with the Step People, even as they stick their swabs right in front of you. They're trying to do their job, not kill you (hopefully), and you will notice that they go about their tasks with a sense of pride and purpose. Just wear some non-skid shoes and watch where you're going!

TALL PEOPLE

Based on my observations, Japanese people have certainly increased in height through the years (I assume this is due to the traditional Japanese diet becoming more westernized with meat and dairy products); still, it is rare to find one over six feet tall. On the other hand, this is not so unusual for Westerners. That said, if you are tall, keep your wits about you (and your helmets handy). There are plenty of opportunities for smashed skulls, ranging from subway exit signs (especially true on the Ginza subway line, Tokyo's first subway line) to doorframes at charming little *kissaten* (coffee/tea shop), where restrooms were apparently built for people the size of E.T.

TAXES

In addition to money taken out of your salary for various taxes (§ "Income Taxes"), you must also pay a municipal tax (*jūminzei*) for living in your ward (*ku*) or city (*shi*). Like your health insurance, the amount you pay is based on your income. It will disturb and upset you, but better get over it now because if you are living/working legally in Tokyo, your "friendly" *kuyakusho* or *shiyakusho* will be sending you constant reminders you have to pay—and pay dearly—for that privilege. Whatever you do, do *not* sign up for automatic withdrawal of your taxes from your bank account. The least you can do is control when (and if) you pay these taxes. (Note: Some wards are "more equal" than other wards, and as a result you have to pay *more* to live in them. Ask around before you get too settled in.)

Also, I strongly recommend that any non-Japanese person reading this book familiarize themselves with the tax laws of their own countries in regards to those who choose to work abroad.

TAXIS (*takushī*)

Be aware when taking a *takushī* (taxi) in Tokyo:

- A taxi with a *red* light in its window means it's available; one with a *green* light means it already has a customer.
- The taxi driver controls the passenger door, meaning: The passenger door will open and close *automatically.* All you do is get in and get out. Do *not* open or close the door!
- Before going anywhere a charge of ¥730 (as of this writing), good for about two kilometers (1.25 miles), pops up on the meter display.

If you are exhausted or have missed the last train and don't live far from where you've finished your last job (or your company is paying for one) take a taxi. They are clean (though some smell like cigarettes), and, generally speaking, the drivers (almost always men) are courteous.

Sometimes the drivers, assuming you speak English, will strike up a conversation. If you're in the mood, this can be a pleasant diversion; if not, you're trapped. If you pretend you don't speak English, you risk either using pidgin English or pidgin Japanese to convey your destination. Either way, you've still used two languages the driver is familiar with. The best way to avoid this is to give the driver your instructions ("Taxi"), immediately whip out your phone and pretend you're having a (long) conversation. This may seem cruel, but otherwise you might end up giving an English lesson—when all you really want to do is to go home and to bed.

TIPS/TIPPING

One great thing about living in Japan is that you don't have to tip anyone in the service industry. (Those of you who have worked in the service industry may not feel the same.) Waitstaff, who are usually paid between ¥800-1,300 an hour, take your order and bring your food (and check) to the table—period, the end. For bellboys who haul your bags up to the room or taxi drivers who drag you across town, you don't open your wallet for anything extra. "Thank you" is all that is required.

TOOTHBRUSHES (*haburashi*)

Another odd choice for "things you should know"? Perhaps. However, except for the overpriced American Pharmacy inside the Marunouchi Building (Marubiru) near Tokyo station, drop me an e-mail if you ever find a Tokyo drugstore that carries a toothbrush that an adult could use. For some reason, toothbrush manufacturers have decided that everyone in Japan has the mouth of a five-year-old child. They are all cute, itsy-bitsy and useless. I wouldn't say that I have a big mouth (others might disagree), but unless I want to brush one tooth at a time, I find that Japanese toothbrushes don't do the trick for me.

TRAVEL RESERVATIONS (§ "Travel")

Do not underestimate the importance of making your travel reservations as far in advance as possible. If it's August and you can remember that Christmas is coming up in December, consider making your reservations right away. You'll be flying home with a smile on your face, safe in the knowledge you won't be spending hours on end trying to find a way to get home (unless you've finally given up and decided that Tokyo *is* home.)

UNDER CONSTRUCTION (*kōji-chū*)

If you have lived in a metropolis, you are aware that construction is ongoing and must be accepted as the price one pays to live in a big city. But even if you live in what one might call the "suburbs" of Tokyo, you must also accept that the sounds of hammers, saws, drills and concrete mixers will disturb every waking hour, making working from home nearly impossible. There is *always* something being torn down or roads being repaired. Safety measures are not necessarily part of the process, so keep your wits about you. Note: If you choose to live in a place that is surrounded by old homes, I can almost guarantee you that as soon as the owner dies, the heirs will sell it and construction work will begin on a 16-unit *manshon* building.

VALENTINE'S DAY/WHITE DAY

You know what Valentine's Day is. But what you don't know is that in Japan, Valentine's Day is "reserved" for women to give men chocolates. This includes *giri-choko*, or "obligatory chocolate"—chocolates that female employees must either give to their bosses or male co-workers (as opposed to *honmei choko*, chocolate reserved for those who are truly loved or desired). But, to make up for all this, on March 14there is "White Day," where the men are supposed to return the favor and buy their gals and office ladies all the fattening *choko* their salaries can afford.

VENDING MACHINES

It is common knowledge that vending machines can be found almost everywhere you go in Japan. And for those that have heard the stories: yes, in addition to canned drinks and cigarettes, you can buy almost anything from vending machines, including bouquets, condoms, business cards and tissues. So, if you go on a blind date in Tokyo and forget the essentials, fear not: somewhere there's a vending machine waiting just for you.

WALKING SLOW

If you find yourself walking behind a pack o' schoolgirls, look for the nearest open space and run for your life. For reasons that remain unclear, these schoolgirls (and sometimes boys) walk as if they're on death row. Not only do they walk slowly, they take up the entire width of any given sidewalk without any remote comprehension there is anyone else in the world who might have to get to an appointment. This style of walking continues all the way into the subway or train station, where even the presence of an oncoming train does not seem to alert any of them to the need to move. Be prepared.

WEATHER (📎 "Weather")

As you will be reminded often, Japan has four distinct seasons. In fact, it actually has five. The fifth is known as *tsuyu* (rainy season), which seems to begin at some point in June and run to some point in July. Downpours can occur at a moment's notice, so it's always best to keep one of those brilliantly compact Japanese umbrellas tucked in your tote unless you want to resemble a wet sheet at day's end. *Tsuyu* can often be followed by sporadic *taifū* (typhoons). *Taifū* can last into September and can be quite nasty. I highly recommend avoiding any air travel during this period. For more information about weather in Japan, make sure you visit the *FIT* website.

WHY DID YOU COME TO JAPAN?

You will certainly be asked this question many times during your "stay" in Japan. Your answer will go through three stages: The first will be relatively honest (i.e. I wanted to take a chance and try a new life); the second will try to curry favor (i.e. I have a deep interest in Japan's culture); and the third might hinge on resignation (i.e. I've been here for so long I don't remember). Decide on a brief answer you are comfortable with and quickly move on.

WINE

If you imbibe, it will soon become apparent that the Japanese believe wine is the nectar of the gods. Perhaps it is, but, in Japan, not only must it be priced accordingly, it must be *served* accordingly. Meaning: If you order a glass of wine in a restaurant, or, worse, in a hotel's restaurant, you will, in fact, be given a *glass*. Whether there is any wine *in* the glass is a matter of opinion. Not being a frequent drinker, I have sat by and watched veins bulge on friends' foreheads when they are served their "glass of wine," only to learn that a glass of wine sometimes means one-half, one-third, or even one-fourth of a glass filled (?) with wine.

Now that you are aware of this situation, I suggest the following methods to cope with it: (1) Accept it. (2) Do as my friend Julian did: Grab the bottle of precious liquid from the hand of the unsuspecting waitstaff, fill your glass to the appropriate height, and say, loud enough for all to hear, "Now *that* is a *glass* of wine!"

❖

JAPANESE 101

Basic Japanese Phrases, Hiragana and Katakana

For those unfamiliar with the Japanese language it might seem daunting to learn any of it. However, upon landing in Tokyo and meeting any number of Westerners speaking Japanese with relative ease, you will discover, as I did, nothing is impossible.

Well, I take that back: I can't teach you how to become fluent in Japanese with this book. I can, though, give a brief introduction to the written language and teach you some basic phrases to enable you to get around the city and meet and greet others. Ready?

As described in "Road Map," Japanese uses three "alphabets" (character sets) for its written language. The most difficult, *kanji,* the multistroke characters, are too complex and time-consuming for this book; your concern is to master the relatively easy *hiragana* and *katakana. Katakana* is used for hundreds of foreign loan words (5) and you will see it on a daily basis throughout Japan, especially in advertisements. As for *hiragana,* as soon as you learn this simple cursive script and some basic vocabulary, you will be able to read some Japanese words that do not require *kanji,* and be able to write simple letters to your new Japanese friends. It's fun to learn this part of the Japanese language and there are a number of online sites that show you exactly how to draw the characters (see § "Japanese Language").

The great thing about Japanese is that the vowel sounds never change, so, even if you cannot understand what you are reading, you are most likely pronouncing it correctly. (Note: If you ever studied Spanish, you'll be way ahead of the game as Japanese and Spanish vowels sound very similar.)

Following is a simple pronunciation chart for Japanese vowel sounds, followed by *hiragana* and *katakana* charts, as well as charts for certain consonant/vowel combinations unique to the Japanese language.

PRONUNCIATION CHART

Japanese has five vowel sounds. In *rōmaji,* they are:

A (あ) like the *a* in *father*
I (い) like the *e* in *see*
U (う) like the *oo* in *too*
E (え) like the *a* in *say*
O (お) like the *o* in *hope*

NOTES:

- Some words have "long" vowel sounds, which, when you read Japanese written in *rōmaji,* are indicated with a macron (¯) over the vowel sound, i.e. *obāsan* (grandmother). This literally means you must stretch the length of the vowel sound slightly.

- The consonant *n* is pronounced as an independent syllable when it follows a vowel, such as in the proper name *Jun'ichirō* (*ju•n•i•chi•ro•u*) or followed by the syllable *ya* as in: *pan'ya* (bread shop), pronounced *pa•n•ya.* (To Western ears, when Japanese is spoken at natural speed, only two syllables will be heard, i.e. *pan'ya.* When Japanese is *sung,* the freestanding *n* syllable is often pronounced clearly.)

- *Fu* is pronounced more like *hu,* so when you say the word "France" in Japanese, instead of it sounding like *furansu,* it will sound more like *huransu.* However, it is still written in *rōmaji* with "f."

- The English "v" becomes "b" in Japanese. So, when the Japanese ask for your *bisa,* they are asking for your *visa.*

- Yes, it's true: In Japan the English "r" and "l" are misunderstood all the time. There is no true "r" or "l" in the Japanese language. So, let's skip the jokes and remain culturally sensitive. The Japanese will laugh at their mistakes if you point them out in a gentle way. So when you hear "*Ai rabu yū,*" you will have to decide if you're about to get a massage or if you just plucked someone's heartstrings (or both).

HIRAGANA ひらがな

Hiragana is the simple cursive script used for basic words, grammatical particles and verb endings, among other uses.

A	あ	**I**	い	**U**	う	**E**	え	**O**	お	**N**	ん
ka	か	ki	き	ku	く	ke	け	ko	こ		
sa	さ	shi	し	su	す	se	せ	so	そ		
ta	た	chi	ち	tsu	つ	te	て	to	と		
na	な	ni	に	nu	ぬ	ne	ね	no	の		
ha	は	hi	ひ	fu	ふ	he	へ	ho	ほ		
ma	ま	mi	み	mu	む	me	め	mo	も		
ya	や			yu	ゆ			yo	よ		
ra	ら	ri	り	ru	る	re	れ	ro	ろ		
wa	わ							wo	を		

KATAKANA カタカナ

Katakana is the angular script used for foreign loan words, foreign names or for emphasis, among other uses.

A	ア	**I**	イ	**U**	ウ	**E**	エ	**O**	オ	**N**	ン
ka	カ	ki	キ	ku	ク	ke	ケ	ko	コ		
sa	サ	shi	シ	su	ス	se	セ	so	ソ		
ta	タ	chi	チ	tsu	ツ	te	テ	to	ト		
na	ナ	ni	ニ	nu	ヌ	ne	ネ	no	ノ		
ha	ハ	hi	ヒ	fu	フ	he	ヘ	ho	ホ		
ma	マ	mi	ミ	mu	ム	me	メ	mo	モ		
ya	ヤ			yu	ユ			yo	ヨ		
ra	ラ	ri	リ	ru	ル	re	レ	ro	ロ		
wa	ワ							wo	ヲ		

To indicate voiced or plosive consonants in *hiragana* or *katakana*, diacritic marks known as *dakuten* (゛) and *handakuten* (゜) are used respectfully, i.e., the "ga" in *gaman* (endurance) would appear as: がまん; the "po" in Pokémon would appear as: ポケモン.

HIRAGANA VOICED CONSONANTS

A	あ	I	い	U	う	E	え	O	お
ga	が	gi	ぎ	gu	ぐ	ge	げ	go	ご
za	ざ	ji	じ	zu	ず	ze	ぜ	zo	ぞ
da	だ	(ji)	ぢ	(zu)	づ	de	で	do	ど
ba	ば	bi	び	bu	ぶ	be	べ	bo	ぼ

HIRAGANA PLOSIVE CONSONANTS

A	あ	I	い	U	う	E	え	O	お
pa	ぱ	pi	ぴ	pu	ぷ	pe	ぺ	po	ぽ

KATAKANA VOICED CONSONANTS

A	ア	I	イ	U	ウ	E	エ	O	オ
ga	ガ	gi	ギ	gu	グ	ge	ゲ	go	ゴ
za	ザ	ji	ジ	zu	ズ	ze	ゼ	zo	ゾ
da	ダ	(ji)	ヂ	(zu)	ヅ	de	デ	do	ド
ba	バ	bi	ビ	bu	ブ	be	ベ	bo	ボ

KATAKANA PLOSIVE CONSONANTS

A	ア	I	イ	U	ウ	E	エ	O	オ
pa	パ	pi	ピ	pu	プ	pe	ペ	po	ポ

To write words requiring palatal sounds (*yōon*, sometimes translated as "diphthong"), combine a consonant (including those marked with *dakuten* or *handakuten*) with a "lower-case" version of *ya*, *yu*, or *yo*. While the resulting combination may sound the same to you, it *isn't*. For example, if you say "***Byo**uin ni itte kudasai*" to a taxi driver, he'll take you to a hospital. But if you say "***Biyou**in ni itte kudasai,*" he'll take you to a beauty salon. Be careful! (i.e. **byo**-u-i-n: hospital; bi-yo-u-i-n: beauty salon)

HIRAGANA PALATAL SOUNDS

Consonant +	***ya***	や	**yu**	ゆ	**yo**	よ
ki (き)	kya	きゃ	kyu	きゅ	kyo	きょ
shi (し)	sha	しゃ	shu	しゅ	sho	しょ
chi (ち)	cha	ちゃ	chu	ちゅ	cho	ちょ
ni (に)	nya	にゃ	nyu	にゅ	nyo	にょ
hi (ひ)	hya	ひゃ	hyu	ひゅ	hyo	ひょ
mi (み)	mya	みゃ	myu	みゅ	myo	みょ
ri (り)	rya	りゃ	ryu	りゅ	ryo	りょ

(with dakuten /handakuten)

Consonant +	***ya***	や	**yu**	ゆ	**yo**	よ
gi (ぎ)	gya	ぎゃ	gyu	ぎゅ	gyo	ぎょ
ji (じ)	jya	じゃ	jyu	じゅ	jyo	じょ
bi (び)	bya	びゃ	byu	びゅ	byo	びょ
pi (ぴ)	pya	ぴゃ	pyu	ぴゅ	pyo	ぴょ

KATAKANA PALATAL SOUNDS

Consonant +	***ya***	ヤ	**yu**	ユ	**yo**	ヨ
ki (キ)	kya	キャ	kyu	キュ	kyo	キョ
shi (シ)	sha	シャ	shu	シュ	sho	ショ
chi (チ)	cha	チャ	chu	チュ	cho	チョ
ni (ニ)	nya	ニャ	nyu	ニュ	nyo	ニョ
hi (ヒ)	hya	ヒャ	hyu	ヒュ	hyo	ヒョ
mi (ミ)	mya	ミャ	my	ミュ	myo	ミョ
ri (リ)	rya	リャ	ryu	リュ	ryo	リョ

(with dakuten/handakuten)

Consonant +	***ya***	ヤ	**yu**	ユ	**yo**	ヨ
gi (ギ)	gya	ギャ	gyu	ギュ	gyo	ギョ
ji (ジ)	jya	ジャ	jyu	ジュ	jyo	ジョ
bi (ビ)	bya	ビャ	byu	ビュ	byo	ビョ
pi (ピ)	pya	ピャ	pyu	ピュ	pyo	ピョ

BASIC JAPANESE PHRASES

These phrases are provided to help you get started from day one in Tokyo. For specific situations (emergencies, etc.), see "Helpful Phrases."

The Japanese phrases are written in *rōmaji,* followed by *hiragana.* (Note: In written Japanese there are usually no spaces after words, only punctuation marks.)

GREETINGS

Good morning.

Ohayō gozaimasu.	おはようございます。

Good afternoon.

Konnichi wa.	こんにちわ。

Good evening.

Konban wa.	こんばんわ。

INTRODUCTIONS

Nice to meet you.

Hajimemashite.	はじめまして。

Please be kind to me.

Dōzo yoroshiku (o-negaishimasu).	どうぞよろしく (おねがいします)。

(Note: the above two phrases are sometimes said together.)

My name is…

________ *to mōshimasu.*	______ ともうします。

What is your name?

O-namae wa nan desu ka?	おなまえはなんですか？

What do you do?

O-shigoto wa nan desu ka?	おしごとはなんですか？

Where are you from?

Go-shusshin wa dochira desuka?	ごしゅっしんはどちらですか？

PLEASE/ THANK YOU

I'd like this/that, please.

Kore/Sore, kudasai.	これ・それ、ください。

Please, come in.

Dōzo, ohairi kudasai.	どうぞ、おはいりください。

Thank you.

Arigatō gozaimasu.	ありがとうございます。

Thank you very much.

Dōmo arigatō gozaimasu.	どうもありがとうございます。

Thank you very much (for having done something).

Dōmo arigatō gozaimashita.	どうもありがとうございました。

RESTAURANTS

Excuse me (I'm ready to order/I need something.)

Sumimasen. [OR] *O-negaishimasu.*	すみません。 おねがいします。

(I'm finished eating and) I'd like the check.

Gochisōsamadeshita.	ごちそうさまでした。

ASKING FOR HELP

Excuse me, but…

Sumimasen ga…	すみませんが、。。。

I can't read kanji. Can you tell me what this/that means?

Kanji ga yomemasen. Kore wa/Sore wa, dō iu imi desuka?	かんじがよめません。これは・それはどういういみですか？

Excuse me (but), can you speak English?

Sumimasen (ga), eigo ga hanasemasuka?	すみませんが、えいごがはなせますか？

Excuse me (but), I'm lost.

Sumimasen (ga), mayotte shimaimashita.	すみませんが、まよってしまいました。

Sorry, my Japanese isn't good. Can you speak English?

Sumimasen ga, watashi no Nihongo wa heta desuga, eigo ga hanasemasuka?	すみませんが、わたしのにほんごはへたですが、えいごがはなせますか。

SUBWAYS/TRAINS

Does this (subway/train) go to…?

Kono chikatetsu/densha wa _____e iku deshō ka?	このちかてつ・でんしゃは___へいくでしょうか?

HOW MUCH (in a store)

How much is this?

Kore wa o-ikura desuka?	これはおいくらですか?

Can I use a credit card?

Kurejitto kādo de yoroshii desuka?	クレジットカードでよろしいですか?

MAGIC WORDS

There are certain words/phrases in Japanese that can be used for a variety of social situations. If you only learn the following Japanese "magic words" and nothing else, you will at least be able to get someone's attention, thank them and indicate your appreciation.

Dōmo arigatō gozaimasu
どうもありがとうございます

This means "thank you very much" (see above for its variations in "Please/Thank You"). You can also just use *dōmo* as a friendly hello/excuse me/thanks to people you see on a regular basis. (You can also combine *dōmo sumimasen* as a sort of excuse, apology or thank you to someone you have inconvenienced.)

Sumimasen
すみません

Sumimasen, and its variations *suimasen* and *sumahen,* is a word which can mean "excuse me"; "pardon me"; and "I'm sorry." Here are situations where you might use it:

- In a shop or restaurant. Saying *sumimasen* signals you are ready for assistance.

- Getting off a subway/train. *Sumimasen* can be used in place of *orimasu* (I will get off) and should alert those nearby that you intend to exit. (Note: You may say this several times during rush hour.)

- When you are late. While there are other phrases you can say, *sumimasen* works as a fast apology.

- As a standard excuse me/pardon me. When bumping into anyone accidentally, *sumimasen* quickly allays fears that you are a big, bad foreigner clueless about proper etiquette.

Yoroshiku o-negaishimasu/O-negaishimasu.
よろしくおねがいします・おねがいします

Yoroshiku o-negaishimasu and *o-negaishimasu* are heard numerous times in any given conversation. Situations may include:

- When you are given a task. In this case, the person asking you to do the task (no matter how large or small) will almost always tag on *yoroshiku o-negaishimasu,* in this case meaning: "I appreciate your kindness (for what you are about to do/for what you are agreeing to do)."

- After you have been introduced to someone. Here, after the initial phrase *hajimemashite* ("Nice to meet you," but literally, "it is starting/beginning") is said, the correct response would be *yoroshiku o-negaishimasu* or *dōzo yoroshiku.* This might translate as "I hope you will be kind to me," or "Please be kind to me."

As mentioned, to get someone's attention in a restaurant or bar you can say "*sumimasen,*" but "*O-negaishimasu*!" will also alert staff that you are ready to order or need assistance.

❖

HELPFUL PHRASES

What I wished I knew how to say before I came to Japan

To help you successfully navigate your way in Tokyo, I have provided helpful phrases for the items below. Recorded versions of them are available via the *FIT* website. If you have never spoken Japanese before, fear not: just refer to the pronunciation tips in the previous chapter, "Japanese 101."

- Auditioning for an Acting or Modeling Job
- Directions
- Being Late
- Taxis
- Getting Paid
- Buying a Ticket for Narita Express
- At a Restaurant
- Shopping for Electronics, Appliances and More
- Point Cards
- Post Office
- Telephone Phrases (General)
- Telephone Phrases (Emergencies)

Recorded phrases are said once in English and twice in Japanese (once at a natural speed, once more slowly). I included the English phrases because most foreign language recordings usually launch into the conversation in the target language. That's fine for some, but I found that having the security of hearing the English phrase once (as opposed to just staring at it in a book) helped "prime" my mind to accept the same phrase in Japanese. Note: There may be some discrepancies between the printed and recorded versions of the phrases, as changes to the text may have occurred between the time the book was published and the time the phrases were recorded. Best efforts were made to ensure exact matches.

AUDITIONING FOR AN ACTING OR MODELING JOB

Most agencies repping foreigners have a fluent English speaker to help set up your auditions—but not always.

If a talent agent calls about an audition, he or she might say:

- Hello. This is Sato at Triple A. There's an audition this Thursday for a new car commercial. Can you make it?
  - *Moshi-moshi. Kochira wa toripuru A no Satō desu. Konshū no moku-yōbi, atarashii kuruma no CM no ōdishon ga arimasu ga, koraremasuka?*
- For now this is just a photo selection. If the client likes your picture we'll call you again and give the audition details at that time.
  - *Ima wa shashin senkou no dankai desu. Kuraianto ga anata no shashin o ki ni ittara, mou ichi do o-denwa o sashiagemasu. Sono toki ni ōdishon no kuwashii koto o o-shiraseshimasu.*

When you hear these phrases, you might reply:

- I might be available on Thursday, but I need to know what time and where.
  - *Hai. Tabun mokuyōbi wa OK desu ga, itsu doko e ikeba yoroshii no deshō ka?*
- Yes, I can make it on Thursday.
  - *Hai. Mokuyōbi wa daijōbu desu.*
- I'm sorry; I can't make it on Thursday.
  - *Zannen desu ga, mokuyōbi wa tsugō ga warui desu.*
- Can you tell me more about the job? Is it in Tokyo? What will I have to do in the commercial?
  - *Mō sukoshi kuwashii koto o oshiete moraemasuka? Bashō wa Tōkyō desuka? CM de wa donna koto o suru no desuka?*

If you don't pass the photo selection, your agent might call and say:

- This is Sato at Triple A.
  - *Toripuru A no Satō desu.*
- I'm sorry; you didn't pass / you failed the photo selection.
  - *Zannen nagara, shashinsenkō ni ukarimasendeshita/ ni ochimashita.*

- When there's another audition, we'll call you.
  - *Mata betsu no ōdishon ga attara, odenwa shimasu.*

If you pass the photo selection, your agent might call and say:

- This is Sato at Triple A. You passed the photo selection!
  - *Toripuru A no Satō desu. Shashinsenkō ni ukarimashita!*
- The audition will be this Thursday between 6 and 8 p.m. near Hanzōmon station.
  - *Ōdishon wa konshū no mokuyōbi, roku-ji kara hachi-ji no aida desu. Hanzōmon eki no chikaku desu.*

If you need to call them to confirm, you can say:

- So, we're meeting this Thursday at 6 p.m. at Hanzōmon station, right? Okay, see you then.
  - *Konshū no mokuyōbi, 6 ji ni, Hanzōmon eki ni ikeba ii no desu ne. De wa, sono toki ni.*

At the audition you will be told to stand near a mark on the floor. A director/production assistant may say:

- Can you speak Japanese?
  - *Nihongo wa hanasemasuka?*
- Please stand here and look at the camera.
  - *Koko ni tatte, kamera o mite kudasai.*
- Say your name and introduce yourself.
  - *O-namae to jikoshōkai o o-negaishimasu.*
- Please turn around slowly.
  - *Yukkuri mawatte mite kudasai.*
- Please show us your profile.
  - *Yokogao o misete kudasai.*

When introducing yourself at the audition, say something like:

- Hi everyone. I'm John Smith and I'm from Los Angeles.
  - *Minasan, konnichi wa. Jon Sumisu desu. Rosu Anjerusu no shusshin desu.*
- I recently appeared in a commercial for a new computer game.
  - *Saikin atarashii conpyūtā gēmu no CM ni demashita.*

- I really enjoy living and working in Japan.
  - *Nihon de no kurashi ga totemo ki ni itte imasu.*
- (And) I'd really like to do this job.
  - *Kono shigoto ga dekitara, ureshii desu.*

You may be shown a storyboard of what you will have to do. You may be asked to perform those actions with the following phrases:

- Please speak a little more slowly / quickly.
  - *Mō sukoshi yukkuri/hayaku hanashite kudasai.*
- Can you please do it a little more slowly / quickly?
  - *Mō sukoshi yukkuri/hayaku dekimasuka?*
- Please show your hands to the camera.
  - *Te o kamera no hō ni mukete kudasai.*
- Please smile so we can see your teeth.
  - *Ha o misete waratte kudasai.*

When you are finished you might hear:

- Thank you.
  - *Arigatō.*
- Thank you for your time and effort.
  - *O-tsukaresama (deshita).**

*An acknowledgment that effort is being made or has been made.

To which you can respond:

- Thank you very much.
  - *Dōmo arigatō gozaimashita.*

DIRECTIONS

When you go for your audition/job interview, you may need to call from a station for further directions. These phrases may help:

- I'm at the south exit of the train station.
  - *Eki no minamiguchi ni imasu.*
- How do I get to your office from here?
  - *Koko kara sochira no ofisu made dō ikeba ii deshōka?*

- Which way should I go?
  - *Dochira e ittara ii desuka?*

The person you are calling might say:

- From where you are you should see an ABC Bank.
  - *Soko kara, ABC ginkō ga mieru deshō.*
- Our office is the next building on the left.
  - *Ofisu wa sono tonari no hidari no biru desu.*

If you explain to the caller where you are calling from, they may say:

- I know where you are.
  - *Anata ga doko ni iru ka wakarimashita.*
- Stay there, please. I'll come and get you.
  - *Soko de matte ite kudasai. Mukae ni ikimasukara.*

If you go to a kōban (police box) to ask for directions, you might say:

- Excuse me. I want to go to the ABC Tower building, but I'm lost.
  - *Sumimasen. ABC Tawā Biru ni ikitai'n desuga, mayotte shimaimashita.*
- I don't know which road to take.
  - *Michi ga wakarimasen.*
- Can you tell me how to get there from here?
  - *Koko kara dō iku ka oshiete kudasai.*

They might show you a map and say:

- Right now, we're here.
  - *Ima, koko ni imasu.*
- Follow this main road for about 200 meters till you see a bread shop on the corner.
  - *Kono ōki na michi o ni hyaku mētoru hodo ittara, kado ni panya ga arimasu.*
- If you turn right there, you'll see the ABC Tower Building.
  - *Sono kado o migi ni magareba, ABC Tawā Biru ga miemasu.*

BEING LATE

As a freelancer, your jobs will sometimes overlap. No one wants to be late, but sometimes it happens. Know what to say.

If you end up arriving late for your appointment, you might say:

- I'm sorry I'm late.
  - *Okurete sumimasen.*
- I'm really sorry for being late.
  - *Mōshiwake arimasen. Okurete shimaimashita.*

If you are running late, you can call ahead and say:

- I'm running a little late.
  - *Chotto okuresō desu.*
- I'll be there as soon as I can.
  - *Dekiru dake hayaku ikimasu no de.*

If your delay is unavoidable due to a transportation problem, you might call ahead to say:

- I'm in the subway station right now.
  - *Ima, chikatetsu no eki ni imasu.*
- They said there will be a delay of ten minutes, so I might be a little late.
  - *Densha ga jyuppun okureru sō desu. Sukoshi okureru to omoimasu.*
- I'm calling from a taxi. Traffic is all backed up.
  - *Takushī kara denwa o shite imasu. Dōro ga jūtai shite imasu.*
- I'll be about ten minutes late.
  - *Jyuppun gurai okureru to omoimasu.*

TAXIS

As a freelancer, you will often take a taxi to an appointment or back home (if you've missed the last train). Here are some phrases to ensure you have a smooth ride:

After you've flagged down a taxi:

- I have a suitcase. Could you open the trunk?
  - *Sutsukesu o motte imasu. Toranku o akete moraemasuka?*

- Please take me to Nogizaka subway station on the Chiyoda line.
  - *Chiyoda-sen no Nogizaka eki e itte kudasai.*
- Do you know where it is?
  - *Go-zonji desuka?*
- I only have ¥10,000 to pay my fare with. Is that okay?
  - *Ichi-man en satsu shika nai'n desu ga, yoroshii desu ka?*

En route you might say to the taxi driver:

- I'm in a rush, so could you please take the fastest route possible? Thanks.
  - *Isoide iru no de, ichiban hayaku ikeru michi o tootte moraemasuka? Arigatō.*
- This street is really crowded.
  - *Kono michi wa konde imasu ne.*
- The traffic isn't moving at all
  - *Zenzen ugokanai yō na no de…*
- Could we take a different street?
  - *Hokano michi o itte moraemasuka?*
- I'm sorry, but this isn't the right street.
  - *Sumimasenga, kono michi ja arimasen.*
- Please don't use this road.
  - *Kono michi wa tooranaide kudasai.*
- There's construction going on and it will take too long.
  - *Kōjichū na no de jikan ga kakatte shimaimasu.*
- Could you please slow down?
  - *Mō sukoshi yūkuri hashitte moraemasuka?*
- Turn left/Turn right at the next corner.
  - *Tsugi no kado de hidari ni/migi ni magatte kudasai.*

The following are things the taxi driver might say to you en route:

- What country are you from?
  - *Dochira no kuni kara irasshaimashitaka?*
- Where are you from?
  - *Doko no kuni kara kita no desuka?*
- How long have you been in Japan?
  - *Dono gurai Nihon ni sunde imasuka?*

- How are you getting along in Japan?
  - *Nihon no kurashi wa dō desuka?*
- How is life in Japan?
  - *Nihon no seikatsu wa dō desuka?*
- Do you like Japanese food?
  - *Nihon no tabemono wa suki desuka?*
- Are you married?
  - *Kekkon shite imasuka?*
- Is your wife Japanese?
  - *Okusan wa Nihon-jin desu ka?*
- Is your husband Japanese?
  - *Go-shujin wa Nihon-jin desu ka?*
- Your Japanese is really good.
  - *Nihongo ga jōzu desu ne!*
- I'm sorry; I can't speak English.
  - *Sumimasen. Eigo ga hanasemasen.*

When it's time to be dropped off, you might say to the taxi driver:

- Please drop me off at the next corner.
  - *Tsugi no kado de oroshite kudasai.*
- Please drop me off in front of that convenience store on the left.
  - *Hidari te no conbini no mae de oroshite kudasai.*
- Please drop me off at that convenience store on the right.
  - *Migi te no conbini no tokoro de oroshite kudasai.*
- Slow down, please, we're almost there.
  - *Mō sugu desu kara, sukoshi supīdo o otoshite kudasai.*
- Here we are. Thank you.
  - *Koko desu. Arigatō.*

GETTING PAID

Always clarify payment details for entertainment jobs. These phrases should help if trouble crops up:

- Excuse me, but can you tell me what the performance fee is for this job?
    - *Sumimasen ga, kono shigoto no gyara wa ikura ka oshiete moraemasuka?*
- So, the payment is ¥15,000 per hour. (Right?)
    - *Shiharai wa jikyū ichi-man go-sen en, desu ne.*
- Is that the before-tax amount or the after-tax amount?
    - *Sore wa zeikomi desuka, tedori desuka?*
- When will I be paid?
    - *Shiharai wa itsu desuka?*
- Okay, let me confirm:
    - *Ja, kakunin sasete kudasai.*
- The after-tax performance fee is ¥15,000 per hour, to be paid on the last day of next month, right?
    - *Gyara wa tedori de jikyū ichi-man go-sen en, shiharai wa raigetsu matsu to iu koto desu ne.*
- Do you have my bank account information?
    - *Watashi no ginkō no kōza bangō ga wakarimasuka?*

If you do not receive the payment for your job as promised, you might call the agency and say:

- Excuse me. You said I'd get paid on the last day of the month, but I didn't receive it yet.
    - *Sumimasenga... sengetsu matsu ni watashi no kyūryō ga furikomareru to kiite imashita ga, mada uketotte imasen.*
- Can you tell me when you're going to transfer the money?
    - *Itsu furikomareru ka oshiete moraemasenka?*
- I'm sorry, but you said I would get paid this month, not next.
    - *Sumimasenga, raigetsu dewa naku, kongetsu shiharatte kureru to iimashita.*
- Could you please send a fax or e-mail confirming the payment amount and payment date?
    - *O-kyūryō no kingaku to shiharai bi o fakkusu ka denshi mēru de okutte moraemasuka?*

- I'd really appreciate it.
  - *Yoroshiku o-negaishimasu.*

The agency may respond as follows:

- We're really sorry.
  - *Mōshiwake arimasen deshita.*
- We changed our payroll system.
  - *Shiharai no hōhō ga kawatta no desu.*
- We'll pay you at the end of next month.
  - *Raigetsu matsu ni o-shiharai shimasu.*
- The client hasn't paid us yet. Could you wait a little longer please?*
  - *Mada, kuraianto ga kochira ni shiharatte imasen. Sukoshi matte itadakemasenka?*

*If this is said with humility, be understanding; unfortunately, it's probably true. Still, don't extend your good graces for more than three months.

- There's been a misunderstanding. It's the pre-tax payment, not the after-tax payment.
  - *Gokai ga atta yō desu ga... Shiharai wa zeikomi desu. Tedori dewa arimasen.*

For most one-time jobs, such as commercials or voice jobs, a transportation fee usually isn't covered. The agent may tell you:

- I'm sorry; we can't pay your transportation.
  - *Mōshiwake arimasen ga, kōtsū hi wa oshiharai dekimasen.*

BUYING A TICKET FOR NARITA EXPRESS

The following phrases will assist you whether you are buying a ticket for the Narita Express (train), the Haneda Express (bus) or Airport Limousine (bus). For Narita Express, you can purchase your ticket up to a month in advance at major train stations, certain travel agencies and reserved seat ticket machines (§ "Narita Airport"). Note: As of this writing, most forms of mass transportation are now smoke-free, but I've listed a helpful phrase to confirm a non-smoking seat, just in case.

Also: as each airport has more than one terminal, confirm which terminal your airline is located at when you purchase your ticket.

When you're ready to buy your ticket, you might say:

- One nonsmoking/smoking seat for Narita Airport please.
  - *Narita kūkō made, ichimai, kin-en seki*/kitsu-en seki o o-negaishimasu.*

    *Note: *Kin-en* means "no smoking"; *kinen* refers to commemoration or prayer. They are *not* pronounced the same.
- Which terminal is ABC Airlines at?
  - *ABC kōkū wa dochira no tāminaru desuka?*
- My flight leaves at 2:55.
  - *Watashi no furaito wa ni ji go-jū-go fun hatsu desu.*
- I'd like to arrive there three hours in advance.
  - *San jikan mae made ni tsukitai desu.*
- I'd like to leave from Shinjuku station.
  - *Shinjuku eki kara o-negaishimasu.*

AT A RESTAURANT

As a freelancer you may spend hours between gigs in restaurants/coffee shops. Below are phrases to help order—and complain.

Note: As mentioned, many restaurants/coffee shops offer "set" meals, which often include a choice of soup/salad, bread/rice, and coffee/tea. For your coffee/tea, specify whether you want it hot or cold. For tea, specify whether you want it with lemon or milk. (If you don't, you'll be asked repeatedly until you do.)

When you're ready to order your meal, you might say to the waitstaff:

- I'll have the "A" set, please, with the soup, the bread and iced lemon tea.
  - *"A" setto de, sūpu to pan to aisu remon tei o o-negaishimasu.*
- Bacon and eggs please.
  - *Bēkoneggu, o-negaishimasu.*
- Make the bacon crispy, please.
  - *Bēkon wa karikari ni yaite kudasai.*

- I'd like the steak. Well done, please.
  - *Sutēki, o-negaishimasu. Uerudan ni shite kudasai.*
- Medium rare, please.
  - *Midiamu rea ni shite kudasai.*
- I'm a vegetarian. Is there any meat in this soup?
  - *Bejitarian na no desuga... kono sūpu wa oniku ga haitte imasuka?*
- I'd like to order something I saw in the window display.
  - *Omise no uindō de oishisō na mono o mimashita*
- I can't read kanji. Can I point it out to you?
  - *Kanji ga yomenai no de, yubi de sashite mo ii desuka?*
- Can you tell me what you *don't* have today?
  - *Kyō chūmon dekinai mono wa arimasuka?*

When you order for yourself and a friend, you might say:

- Excuse me. When the food is ready, could you bring our meals at the same time?*
  - *Sumimasen ga, ryōri wa dōji ni hakonde kuremasenka?*

(*When two people order a meal in a small restaurant, the waitstaff may bring one while the other is being prepared. This phrase may encourage the staff to bring both meals at once.)

When you've given your order to the waitstaff, they might say to you:

- I'm sorry; we're out of that today.
  - *Mōshiwake arimasen. Kyō wa mō owarimashita.*
- Do you want your drink before / after / with your meal?
  - *O-nomimono wa o-shokuji no mae ni / ato ni shimasu ka? / issho ni o-mochi shimashōka?*

When you need to request other things, you might say to the waitstaff:

- Excuse me, could I have more water please?
  - *Sumimasen, o-mizu o mō ippai kudasai.*
- Excuse me, I need a fork / knife / spoon / chopsticks / napkin.
  - *Sumimasen ga, fōku/naifu/supūn o-hashi o kudasai.*
- May I have a refill (of this coffee)?
  - *Kōhī no o-kawari itadakemasuka?*

- Are the refills free?
  - *O-kawari wa jiyū desuka?*

When you have problems with the service, you might say:

- Excuse me. We ordered 20 minutes ago. Isn't it ready yet?
  - *Sumimasen. Ni-jyūppun mae ni chūmon shimashita ga, mada desuka?*
- This isn't what I ordered.
  - *Kore wa chūmon shita mono to chigaimasu.*
- I asked for coffee, not tea.
  - *Watashi wa kōcha de wa naku, kōhī o chūmon shimashita.*

When you're finished eating, the waitstaff might say:

- Is it okay if I take this away?
  - *O-sageshite yoroshii desuka?*

Thirty minutes before closing, the waitstaff might say:

- It's time for the last order.
  - *Rasuto ōdā desu.*
- Would you like anything else?
  - *Go-chūmon wa hoka ni arimasenka?*

If you have any complaints, you might say:

- Excuse me, the background music is a little loud…
  - *Sumimasen. BGM ga sukoshi ōkii no desu ga...*
- Could you turn it down a little?
  - *Chiisaku shite moraemasuka?*
- I'm sorry, but this doesn't taste right.
  - *Sumimasen ga, chotto hen na aji ga shimasu.*
- Could you bring me another one?
  - *Betsu na mono to torikaete moraemasuka?*
- Can I sit someplace else?
  - *Seki o kaete mo ii desuka?*
- This food is cold.
  - *Kono o-ryōri wa samete imasu.*
- I asked for this to be prepared well done. It's rare.
  - *Uerudan de onegaishimashita ga, rea desu.*

- Can I have this prepared well done?
  - *Uerudan ni yaite moraemasuka?*

If you are sitting near others who start smoking in a non-smoking area, you might say:

- Excuse me. Would you please mind not smoking here?
  - *Sumimasenga, tabako o suwanaide itadakemasuka?*

When it's time for you to pay (the cashier), you might hear:

- Okay, that's ¥10,000.
  - *Ichi man en itadakimasu.*
- Thank you for waiting.
  - *Omatase-shimashita.*
- Your change is ¥7, 000.
  - *Nana sen en no o-tsuri desu.*
- Thank you very much.
  - *Dōmo arigatō gozaimashita.*

Shopping for Electronics, Appliances and More

(§ "Electronics / Appliances")

Shopping for electronics, etc., is usually done at big chain stores (like Yodobashi Camera). Although some of these stores employ bilingual employees, it is still to your benefit to know some key phrases:

When you're trying to find a particular item, you might ask a store employee:

- Is there an English-speaking person available?
  - *Koko ni eigo o hanaseru kata ga irasshaimasuka?*
- Okay, well. My Japanese isn't so good, but I'll try to explain what I want.
  - *Sō desuka? Watashi no nihongo wa amari umaku arimasenga, setsumei shite mimasu.*
- Do you have printer cartridges?
  - *Purintā no kātorijji wa arimasuka?*
- Do you have A4-size paper?
  - *A4 saizu no yō shi wa arimasuka?*

- Do you have batteries for wristwatches?
  - *Ude-dokei no denchi wa arimasuka?*
- Where are they? [Where is it?]
  - *Doko ni arimasuka?*
- Can you show me where they're located? [...where it's]
  - *Annai shite itadakemasuka?*

If you find the item you want, you might ask a store employee:

- I'd like to buy this please. Do you have the same thing in stock?
  - *Kore o kaitai no desu ga... kore to onaji mono ga arimasuka?*

If the item isn't available, the store employee might say:

- We don't have any in stock right now.
  - *Tadaima, zaiko ga arimasen.*
- Sorry. We're sold out.
  - *Mōshiwake arimasen. Urikiremashita.*
- Sorry. Unfortunately, this is the last one.
  - *Mōshiwake arimasen. Zannen nagara, kore dake desu.*

If you want to order an item that has been sold-out, you might say:

- Could you order it for me?
  - *Chūmon shite itadakemasuka?*

The store employee might respond as follows:

- Yes, I can order it for you.
  - *Hai. Chūmon itashimasu.**
- I'm sorry, I can't.
  - *Mōshiwake arimasen. Dekimasen.*

* *Itashimasu* is the humble version of *shimasu*, "to do."

If they can order it for you, you might ask them:

- How long will it take to get it?
  - *Dono gurai kakarimasuka?*
- How much does it cost?
  - *O-ikura desuka?*
- Could you call or e-mail me to tell me the item has arrived?
  - *Todoitara, denwa ka "E"mēru o itadakemasuka?*

- Do I need to pay for it now?
  - *Shinamono no o-shiharai wa ima deshō ka?*
- Is it OK to pay for it when I come back here to get it?
  - *Shinamono o uketori ni kita toki ni shiharatte ii deshō ka?*

If the display item is the only one available and you want to buy it, you might say:

- May I have a discount?
  - *Waribiki o shite itadakemasuka?*

If you have questions about English-language manuals, warranties, or repairs, you might ask:

- Does this come with an English-language manual?
  - *Kore ni wa eigo no setsumei-sho ga tsuite imasuka?*
- Can you order an English-language manual for this?
  - *Kore yō no eigo no setsumei-sho o chūmon shite moraemasuka?*
- Does this come with a warranty?
  - *Kore ni wa hoshō ga tsuite imasuka?*
- How many years is the warranty good for?
  - *Sono hoshō wa nan nen yūkō desuka?*
- Is the warranty good overseas or just for Japan?
  - *Sono hoshō wa kaigai de mo yūkō desuka? Nihon dake desuka?*
- Do you sell any products which have an international warranty?
  - *Kaigai demo yūkō na hoshō no tsuita seihin ga arimasuka?*
- If I need to get this repaired, can I bring it back to this shop?
  - *Shūri ga hitsuyō na toki ni nattara, kono o-mise de naoshite moraemasuka?*
- If not, where can I go?
  - *Moshi dame nara, doko e motte ikeba ii desuka?*

Point Cards, Receipts and Bags

When it's time to pay for purchases in Japan, streamline your checkout experience by knowing what to say to deal with *pointo kādo* (point cards), receipts and plastic bags.

If the store you're at offers point cards, and you'd like to get one, you might say:

- How can I get a point card for this store?
  - *Kono o-mise no pointo kādo o morau ni wa dō shitara ii no desuka?*
- Can you make one for me?
  - *Tsukutte itadakemasuka?*

To get the point card, you may have to show your Alien Registration Card and fill out a form. A staff member might say:

- Do you have your alien registration card?
  - *Gaikokujin tōrokushō o motte imasuka?*
- Could you write down your name, address and phone number?
  - *Koko ni o-namae to go-jūsho to denwa bangō o kaite itadakemasuka?*
- And then sign, please.
  - *Sore kara, sain o o-negaishimasu.*

After you have received your card and it's time to pay for your purchases, the cashier might say:

- Do you have a point card?
  - *Pointo kādo wa o-mochi desuka?*
- How do you want to use your points?
  - *Pointo o o-tsukai ni narimasuka?*

You can respond to the cashier with the following phrases:

- I'd like to keep my points.
  - *Pointo o tametai desu.*
- I'd like to use all my points.
  - *Pointo o zenbu tsukaitai desu.*
- I'd like to use 100 of my points.
  - *Pointo o 100 pointo dake tsukaitai desu.*

If you've forgotten or lost your point card, you might say:

- I'm sorry; I left my point card at home.
  - *Suimasen, ie ni pointo kādo o oite kite shimaimashita.*

- I'm sorry; I forgot it.
  - *Suimasen.* Wasurete kite shimaimashita.*
- I lost my point card.
  - *Pointo kādo o nakushite shimaimashita.*
- How can I get another one?
  - *Atarashii no o tsukuritai no desu ga…*

*Variant of *sumimasen.*

After you have paid for your purchase, you're often given your receipt and change at the same time. If you'd like the receipt in the bag, you can say:

- Could you put the receipt in the bag?
  - *Ryōshūsho wa kono fukuro no naka ni irete moraemasuka?*

When you plan to hand-carry the item you've purchased or when you've brought your own bag with you, you might say:

- I don't need a bag.
  - *Fukuro wa irimasen.*
- Like that is fine, thank you.
  - *Sono mama de ii desu.*

POST OFFICE

As mentioned in "Things You Should Know," going to the post office in Tokyo can be a challenge. Avoid those temper tantrums with these helpful phrases:

When you speak to a post office clerk, you might say:

- How much is an airmail stamp to send a postcard overseas?
  - *Gaikoku ni dasu e-hagaki no kitte wa o-ikura desuka?*
- I see. May I have ten postcard stamps please?
  - *Wakarimashita. Sore o jyū mai kudasai.*
- This envelope only contains a letter.
  - *Kono fūtō no nakami wa tegami dake desu.*
- Isn't this just a standard size envelope?
  - *Kono fūtō wa teikei no saizu de wa nai no desuka?*

- That seems expensive.
  - *Chotto takai mitai desu.*
- Do you have any tape or glue?
  - *Tēpu ka nori wa arimasuka?*
- I'd like a receipt, please.
  - *Ryōshūsho o o-negaishimasu.*
- I want this sent by **special delivery**.
  - *Kore o* ***sokutatsu**** *de okuritai no desu ga...*
  - *(*Sokutatsu means next day delivery within Japan.)*
- Can I get this delivered today?
  - *Kyōjyū ni haitatsu suru koto ga dekimasuka?*
- There's a breakable item in this envelope.
  - *Kono fūtō no naka ni wa kowaremono ga haitte imasu.*
- Do you have a "fragile" label we can put on this?
  - *Toriatsukai chūi no shi-ru o hatte moraemasuka?*

The following conversation is typical of one you may have with a post office clerk (A: Post Office Clerk/B: You)

- **A:** What's in this envelope?
  - *Kono fūtō no naka ni wa nani ga haitte imasuka?*
- **B:** A letter.
  - *Tegami desu.*
- **A:** Is there anything else other than a letter inside?
  - *Naka ni wa tegami no hoka ni nani ka haitte imasuka?*
- **B:** Just a letter
  - *Tegami dake desu.*
- **A:** May I open this envelope?
  - *Kono fūtō o akete mo ii desuka?*
- **B:** Sure. Go ahead
  - *Hai. Dōzo.*

Additional phrases you might hear from the postal staff:

- Please go to Window # 4 for express mail / special delivery.
  - *Sokutatsu wa yon-ban no madoguchi e itte kudasai.*
- ... registered mail / registered letters.
  - *... genkinkakitome/kakitome yūbin*
- (Before we mail this) Please fill out this form.*
  - *Kono shorui ni kinyū shite kudasai.*

- Please go to Window #7 to pay the utility bill. **
  - *Kōnetsu hi no furikomi wa nana-ban mado guchi e itte kudasai.*

*If you're given a customs form, it may be in French or Japanese.
**Japanese post offices also offer banking services.

TELEPHONE

Success as a freelancer in Tokyo often depends on your ability to communicate in Japanese on the phone. Following are phrases to get you going:

Work-related

The following phrases will help you inquire about a job on the phone:

- Is an English-speaking person available?
  - *Eigo ga hanaseru kata wa irasshaimasuka?*
- My Japanese isn't so good, but...
  - *Watashi no Nihongo wa heta desu kedo,*
- I'm calling about the classified ad I saw in today's Japan Times.
  - *Kyō no Japan Taimuzu no kōkoku o mite, o-denwa shimashita.*
- Yes, I can come in for an interview today.
  - *Hai. Kyō, mensetsu ni ukagaemasu.*
- Can you send me a map to your office by fax or e-mail?
  - *Sochira no ofisu made no chizu o fakkusu ka* "E" *mēru de okutte moraemasuka?*
- Shall I tell you my e-mail address?
  - "E" *mēru no adoresu o oshiemashōka?*
- By the way, you can see my résumé on my website.
  - *Tokoro de, watashi no rirekisho wa watashi no uebusaito de miru koto ga dekimasu.*
- Can you tell me a little about the job over the phone?
  - *Denwa de shigoto no naiyō o sukoshi o-hanashi shite moraemasuka?*

When you're trying to connect with the person in charge, you might hear and say the following: (A: You / B: Company)

- A: (Please connect me with the) person in charge of the personnel department.
  - *Jinji tantō suru hito o o-negaishimasu.*

- B: What is the purpose of your call?
  - *Donna go-yōken deshō ka?*
- A: I'm very interested in your company and I'd like to work for you.
  - *Kisha ni taihen kyōmi o mochi, shigoto o shitai'n desu ga...*
- B: Just a moment, please. (OR) I'll connect you with the person in charge.
  - *Shōshō o-machi kudasai. (OR) Tantō-sha ni o-tsunagi shimasu.*

General phrases

When trying to reach another party, you might say:

- I received a phone message from Mr. Yamada yesterday...
  - *Kinō, Yamada-san kara rusu ni denwa o itadaita no desu ga...*
- Is he there?
  - *Irasshaimasuka?*
- This is important, so, may I wait?
  - *Daiji na koto na no de, matte mo ii desuka?*

If the party you wish to speak to is unavailable, you might hear:

- I'm sorry.
  - *Mōshiwake arimasen.*
- The line is busy now.
  - *Ima wa hanashichū desu*
- He can't come to the phone now.
  - *Denwa ni deru koto ga dekimasen.*
- He went out.
  - *Dekakete imasu.*
- He's out of the office.
  - *Gaishutsu shite imasu.*
- He's away from his desk.
  - *Seki o hazushite orimasu.*
- He's on the phone.
  - *Denwachū desu.*
- He's in a meeting.
  - *Kaigichū desu.*
- He's in a meeting right now.
  - *Tadaima, kaigichū de gozaimasu.**

  * *de gozaimasu* is a humble form of *desu* (to be / to exist).

- He's on holiday.
  - *Kyūkachū desu.*
- He's out to lunch.
  - *Chūshoku ni dekakete imasu.*
- Do you want to wait?
  - *Shibaraku o-machi itadakemasuka?*
- Shall I take a message?
  - *Dengon o itashimashōka?*

If you need the other party to contact you, you might say:

- Please take a message.
  - *Dengon o o-negaishimasu.*
- Please tell (ask) Mr. Yamada to call me back.
  - *Yamada-san ni o-denwa itadakitai'n desu ga…*
- I'll call again.
  - *Mō ichi do o-denwa shimasu.*
- When is a good time to call again?
  - *Nanji goro o-kake sureba yoroshii deshō ka?*
- When will Mr. Yamada be in the office?
  - *Yamada-san wa itsu kaisha ni irasshaimasuka?*
- Please give Mr. Yamada my regards.
  - *Yamada-san ni yoroshiku otsutae kudasai.*

When you want to confirm or change appointments over the phone:

- I'd like to confirm my appointment with Ms. Suzuki tomorrow at 10:00 a.m.
  - *Ashita gozen jyū ji ni Suzuki-san to o-aisuru apointo no kakunin o shitai no desu ga…*
- I have an appointment with Mr. Yamada this Friday at 2:00. Can we change it to 3:00?
  - *Konshū no kinyōbi ni ji ni Yamada-san to apointo ga arimasu. Sore o san ji ni henkō dekimasu ka?*

When someone has called to confirm if another person has contacted you:

- Has Mr. Kanematsu called you?
  - *Kanematsu-san kara denwa ga arimashita ka?*

When calling a residence (A: Caller/B: Other Party):

- **A:** Is this the Satoh residence?
  - *Satō-san no otaku desu ka?*
- **B:** Yes it is. Who's calling please?
  - *Hai, sō desu. Dochira-sama deshō ka?*
- **A:** My name is... I'd like to speak to your husband / wife.
  - *Watashi no namae wa... go-shujin/okusama o-negaishimasu.*

Miscellaneous telephone phrases:

- I lost her phone number.
  - *Kanojo no denwa bangō o nakushimashita.*
- May I use the phone?
  - *Denwa shite mo ii desu ka?*
- The phone is ringing.
  - *Denwa ga natte imasu.*
- Could you answer the phone?
  - *Denwa ni dete kuremasuka?*
- I'll get the phone.
  - *Denwa o torimasu.*
- Extension 300, please.
  - *Naisen no san-byaku ban o o-negaishimasu.*
- Sorry. I dialed the wrong number.
  - *Dōmo sumimasen. Machigaemashita.*
- You've got the wrong number.
  - *Iie, chigaimasu.*
- I'd like to speak to Ms. Watanabe, please.
  - *Watanabe-san to hanashitai no desu ga, onegai dekimasuka...*
- Could you speak more slowly please?
  - *Mō sukoshi yukkuri hanashite moraemasuka?*
- Thank you for calling so many times.
  - *Nankai mo o-denwa o arigatō gozaimasu.*

TELEPHONE PHRASES FOR EMERGENCIES

(§ "Telephone Emergencies")

These phrases are also on the *FIT* website. Print and memorize.

The word *kare* can be used for boyfriend/husband; *kanojo* can be used for girlfriend/wife; *hito* is (a/some) person, and *tomodachi* is (gender-neutral) friend. Pronouns are not always used in Japanese. "*Kega o shimashita*" could mean: "I am/He/She is injured." Also, refer to yourself as "*Watashi **wa**...*"; others as "*Tomodachi **ga**...*". *Wa* and *ga* are subject markers. See the *FIT* website, "Japanese Language Study."

For emergencies, dial 119. For police, dial 110.

- Help me please!
  - *Tasukete kudasai!*
- There's a fire!
  - *Kaji desu!*
- Send an ambulance! Please hurry!
  - *Kyūkyusha o o-negaishimasu! Isoide kudasai!*
- Please call a policeman!
  - *Omawarisan o yonde kudasai!*

The operator might say:

- What happened?
  - *Dō shimashitaka?*
- To who?
  - *Dare desuka?*
- Where do you live?
  - *Jūsho wa doko desuka?*

You might say:

- My friend is unconscious.
  - *Tomodachi no ishiki ga arimasen.*
- I've suddenly become ill. I need to see a doctor immediately.
  - *Watashi **wa** kyūbyō desu. Ima sugu ni, isha ni mite moraitai no desu.*

- My friend has suddenly become ill. He needs to see a doctor immediately.
  - *Tomodachi* ***ga*** *kyūbyō desu. Ima sugu ni, isha ni mite moraitai no desu.*
- My friend stopped breathing.
  - *Tomodachi ga iki o shite imasen.*
- I burnt my hand.
  - *Te ni yakedo o shimashita.*
- My friend burnt his hand.
  - *Tomodachi* ***ga*** *te ni yakedo o shimashita.*
- My friend has collapsed.
  - *Tomodachi ga taorete imasu.*
- I'm / My friend is injured.
  - *Watashi* ***wa****/Tomodachi* ***ga*** *kega o shimashita.*
- I'm / My friend is bleeding (heavily).
  - *Watashi* ***wa****/Tomodachi* ***ga*** *daishukketsu shite imasu.*
- My name is... My address is... My phone number is... My home is near a convenience store.
  - *Watashi no namae wa... Jūsho wa... denwa bangō wa... ie no soba ni wa conbini ga arimasu.*

CAVEATS

What I learned... the hard way

FIT

In the process of completing *FIT*, transportation fares have risen, immigration procedures have changed, technology has advanced, and Japanese prime ministers have come and gone... and come and gone again. The point: I have made every effort to ensure the information presented in *FIT* (and on its website) is accurate, but I cannot assume responsibility for things that have changed. Also, links on the *FIT* website may contain third-party information and links to other Internet sites, none of which I can take responsibility for. In other words: I have done my best to provide you with valid information, but it is up to you to confirm or verify that information and proceed accordingly.

Falling in Love

If you are unattached, you, like many others who have come to Japan, might fall in love with a Japanese national. I did, and so did 95% of my Western freelancing-in-Tokyo friends. This clearly must be a good thing, so be aware that by coming here you might open a door to a life you never imagined, a life that might include living many more years in Japan than you had anticipated. This could be the greatest thing that ever happened to you, but it also might mean decades of flying back and forth between two sets of families and friends. At a certain point it may become difficult to continue splitting your life between two countries. I'm just saying have an awareness of this situation, as it may not have been part of your life plan. (Love is funny that way.)

Starting Life Over Again

Without realizing it, you can become a "new" person in Tokyo. Change your name, hair color, life story—who would know? A new job, new place to live, new friends and new language all create a "new you." For many who have experienced difficulties in life, this "fresh start" is an incredible opportunity. Alternatively, you may be perfectly happy with who you are. If you come to Japan and stay for any length of time, though, some kind of personal change is unavoidable. I say it's a good thing—but it's your life, so think about it.

I want to go home!

At some point during your Tokyo adventure, you may wake up one day feeling frustrated with situations over which you have no control. You will say, "Get me out of here!" Every Westerner I have met gets to this point and so will you. However, what will happen is this: Many of you will go home, stay for a while, and think: *Why am I here?* And you will promptly get on the next plane and come back to Japan—even if you have to start all over again! I have done it, several close friends have done it and friends of friends have done it.

Once you sheepishly return to Japan and pretend that you just went back for a "visit," you will be forced to take whatever jobs you can get—which, for many of you, will still pay more than what you would have made in your own country.

Do not make any emotional decisions to leave or race back here. Take time to think things out; you will be glad you did.

Life outside of Tokyo

It would be sad if your only experience of Japan were coming to Tokyo just to make as much money as possible. Remember, Japan is a country rich in history and tradition. There is much to learn and explore, so make sure you do so. Visit Kyoto, Osaka, Nagoya, Sapporo. Try an *onsen,* take a calligraphy class, climb Mt. Fuji—the list of suggestions is endless. Yes, you may learn about Japan's tragic past and read about disturbing things. But you will also encounter moments of beauty that you cannot compare to anything in your Western experience. It is certainly a combination of these accumulated moments that are part of the reason why I have returned to Japan so many times. I now feel Japan is part of my life; living here has forever altered my perception of myself, and, to quote my friend (and first Japanese teacher) Ritsuko Arisaka, "I now see the world through two sets of glasses," each with its own distinct, brilliant view. Beyond the monetary rewards, this new way to see the world is one of the things I hope you will gain from your freelancing in Tokyo experience.

❖

CONTACTS

From my little black book…

Following is a very short list of agencies that I or others I know have worked for. I have not listed agents' names. Unless an agent owns the agency, most move on after a few years. Your job is to call the agency and introduce yourself. **DO NOT** use my name as a reference; it serves no purpose. If an agency calls me and asks why you are saying I referred you, I will be forced to remove the agency's name from *FIT*'s website, and future *FIT* readers will lose out on what may be a valuable contact.

Check the *FIT* website for updates. Listings were valid as of this writing. (See § "Talent Agencies") (Note: "P" is phone, "F" is fax and "all" means all types represented.)

Art Quest (*voice actors*) artquest.jp
P (03) 3940-1795 • F (03) 3940-1797

Bright-Aki Co. (*voice actors*) bright-aki.co.jp
P (03) 5474-7456 • F (03) 5474-7457

DAG Music (*voice actors/singers/musicians*) dagmusic.com
P (03) 3423-9665 • F (03) 5474-3135

Dxim (d-ZHYME) (*all*) dxim.biz/en
P (03) 3407-6505 • F (03) 3407-6506

Free Wave (*all*) f-w.co.jp/e/index.html
P (03) 3467-4311 • F (03) 3467-4312

IST (*voice actors*) ist-tokyo.jp/jobs
P (03) 5449-3961 • F (03) 5449-3962

Kaz Planning, Inc. (*wedding musicians*) kaz-planning.com
P (03) 3465-8572 • F (03) 3465-8571

Latina Int'l Corp. (*voice actors*) latinacorp.com
P (03) 3460-8443 • F (03) 3460-8477

Lint (*voice actors/writers*) lint.co.jp
P (03) 3419-9301

Lui, Inc. (*singers, musicians*) lui-inc.com
P (03) 5706-3200 • F (03) 5706-3100

Macmillan Language House (*voice actors*) mlh.co.jp
P (03) 5227-3584 • F (03) 5227-3585

Obunsha Enterprises (*voice actors*) obunsha.co.jp
P (03) 3266-6400

TPS (*voice actors*) tps-inc.jp
P (03) 3443-9361 • F (03) 3443-9362

Yokoh Music Office (*musicians*) yokohmusic.com
P (03) 3574-0531 • F (03) 3574-0631

Zenith (*actors/models*) zenithinc.jp / index.html
P (03) 5411-7747 • F (03) 5411-2527

RESOURCES

Be prepared.

HELPFUL PHONE NUMBERS

The following phone numbers were valid as of this writing. An **[E]** indicates English-speaking personnel should be available. However, when calling 119 (Ambulance/Emergency/Fire) or 110 (burglaries/non-injury traffic accidents), even if there is an English-speaking operator available, *do not expect them to speak it fluently*. Attempts may also be made to connect you to an interpreter if the operator is unable to assist. In the meantime, speak slowly and clearly, and *do not* hang up the phone until after the operator does. To be safe, always have a copy of *FIT*'s Telephone Emergencies phrases. (See: "Helpful Phrases.")

• **Ambulance/Emergency/Fire: 119 (*ichi-ichi-kyū*)**

Ambulances are free of charge, but any medical procedures that are carried out while you (or your loved one) are in one are chargeable. Familiarize yourself with the hospitals/clinics nearest to where you work/live, and be prepared to tell the ambulance driver to take you there, i.e. *Shinjuku no ABC Byōin ni itte kudasai.* (Please take me to the ABC Hospital in Shinjuku.) However, based on your location, ambulance personnel will ultimately determine where you will be taken.

Also, if you have Japanese health insurance, make sure you have your (Japanese) National Health Insurance card (*hokenshō*) on you, as well as your Alien Registration Card (*gaikokujin tōroku-shomeishō*) and/or any pertinent information written down in Japanese so it can be handed to ambulance personnel. If you do not have Japanese health insurance, make sure you consult with your private insurance company to know what documents you require and/or what procedures you need to follow in case you experience an emergency while living here.

Note: *Do not expect ambulance personnel to break down your door and save you!* If you live alone, do your best to alert your neighbor(s) to your condition. Someone is expected to stand outside the building in which you live to "greet" the ambulance personnel (hint: all the more reason for you to be friendly with the people around you). Once inside the ambulance, *do not expect the paramedics to save your life!* Japanese "paramedics" are basically firefighters, not EMTs (Emergency Medical Technicians). Antiquated laws severely restrict what they are able to do to save someone's life. It is only as of April 1, 2006 that they were allowed to administer drugs for cardiac arrest. Essentially, their main purpose is to try to get you to a hospital. Sad, but true.

- **AMDA Int'l Medical Info Center of Japan**: (03) 5285-8088 **[E]**
  M-F 9am-5pm. Introduction to medical facilities with staff who can speak English and explain the Japanese health care system.

- **Emergency Interpretation Service**: (03) 5285-8185 **[E]**
  M-F 5pm-8pm; Weekends & Holidays 9am-8pm. This service is for foreign patients in Japanese hospitals who require English language assistance in situations where treatment is not being handled smoothly. Phone interpretation service is also available when communication problems prevent institutions from providing emergency care to foreign nationals during the following hours: M-F 5-10pm; Weekends & Holidays 9am-10pm.

- **Fire/Ambulance/Emergency: 119**

- **(Tokyo) Fire Department (03) 3212-2323**

- **Japan Help**: 01-2046-1997 **[E]**
  Inquiries to Police & Fire Department, available 24 hours

- **Police: 110 (Japanese), (03) 3501-0110 or 9110** [E]
  Mon-Fri 8:30am-5:15pm

- **(Tokyo) Police (Tsūyaku Center) (03) 3581-4321**
  24 hours a day (*tsūyaku* means interpretation/translation)

- **Tokyo Metropolitan Health & Medical Information Center**
  (*Tokyo-to Hoken Iryo Joho Sentā*): (03) 5285-8181 **[E]**
  From 9am-8pm daily. Referrals to medical institutions where treatment is available in a foreign language.

CLINICS/HOSPITALS

There are supposedly English-speaking staff at the following facilities, but don't count on it. In other words, the English-speaking individual(s) may not be on duty when you call. My experience with this has been hit and miss. The one phrase you must memorize is: *Eigo ga hanaseru hito wa irasshaimasuka?* (Is an English-speaking person available?)

Also, do *not* expect to get an appointment. You *may* be able to get one (or at least a block of time during which to come), but generally speaking, visiting a hospital or a clinic is tantamount to attending a cattle call audition. Advice: Bring a good book.

In addition, some hospitals are unwilling to see you on a national holiday. This is when you call places like the National Medical Clinic (listed below), a *gaijin*-friendly clinic in Hiroo (a neighborhood heavily populated with expats). This is what I did on one such occasion. The National Medical Clinic was open, took me right away and gave me appropriate medicine. Note: At clinics such as these, where the doctors speak English and the clientele consists mainly of non-Japanese, you will most likely be expected to pay cash for an office visit; no insurance, national or foreign, is accepted.

Clinics/Hospitals

- Keio University Hospital
  P (03) 3353-1211 hosp.keio.ac.jp/english/index_uc.htm
  35 Shinanomachi, Shinjuku-ku, Tokyo 160-8582

- International Catholic Hospital (Seibo Byoin)
  P (03) 3951-1111 seibokai.or.jp/english.html
  2-5-1 Nakaochiai, Shinjuku-ku, Tokyo 161-8521

- International Medical Center of Japan
  P (03) 3202-7181 **[E]** imcj.go.jp/dcc/dcc-e/index-e.html
  1-21-1 Toyama, Shinjuku-ku, Tokyo 162-8655

- National Medical Clinic
  P (03) 3473-2057 **[E]** nmclinic.net
  #202, 5-16-11 Minami-Azabu, Minato-ku, Tokyo 106-0047

- Sanno Hospital
  P (03) 3402-2187 **[E]** sannoclc.or.jp
  8-10-16 Akasaka, Minato-ku, Tokyo 107-0052

- St. Luke's International Hospital
  P (03) 3541-5151 **[E]** luke.or.jp/eng/index.html
  9-1 Akashi-cho, Chuo-ku, Tokyo 104-8560

- Tokai Univ. Tokyo Hospital
  P (03) 3370-2321 tokai.ac.jp/tokyohosp
  1-2-5 Yoyogi, Shibuya-ku, Tokyo 151-0053

- Tokyo Adventist Hospital
  P (03) 3392-6151 **[E]** tokyoeisei.com
  3-17-3 Amanuma, Suginami-ku, Tokyo 167-8507

- Tokyo Medical Clinic
  P (03) 3436-3028 tmsc.gr.jp
  No. 32 Mori Bldg. 3-4-30 Shiba Koen
  Minato-ku, Tokyo 105-0011(Closed after 1pm on Sat/Sun)

- Tokyo Women's Medical University Hospital
  P (03) 3353-8111 twmu.ac.jp/info-twmu/index.html
  8-1 Kawada-cho, Shinjuku-ku, Tokyo 162-8666

- Tokyo Women's Medical University, Daini Hospital
  P (03) 3810-1111
  2-1-10 Nishiogu, Arakawa-ku, Tokyo 116-8567

ADDITIONAL USEFUL PHONE NUMBERS

- American Chamber of Commerce
  P (03) 3433-5381 accj.or.jp
  Masonic 39 Mori Bldg. 10F
  2-4-5 Azabudai, Minato-ku, Tokyo 106-0041

- American Embassy
  P (03) 3224-5000, (03) 3224-5174 tokyoacs.com
  1-10-5 Akasaka Minato-ku Tokyo 107

- Electric Company
  P (03) 3501-8111 **[E]**

- Foreign Labor Rights Lawyers
  P (03) 3357-5506 (10am-5pm) **[E]**

- Foreign Residents' Advisory Center
  P (03) 5320-7744 **[E]** Mon-Fri 9:30am-4pm (Except 12-1)

- Foreign Section of the Tokyo Regional Tax Bureau
  P (03) 3216-6811 **[E]**
  nta.go.jp/taxanswer/english/gaikoku.htm
  Mon-Fri 9am-12pm/1-5pm

- Fusion/GOL (ISP)
  P 0120-987-800 (free dial) home.gol.com/english

- Gas Company:
  P (03) 3433-2111 **[E]**
  Mon-Fri 10am-4pm

- Immigration
  P (03) 5796-7111/5796-7112 **[E]** moj.go.jp/ENGLISH
  5-5-30 Konan, Minato-ku, Tokyo
  Mon-Fri 9am-12pm/1-4pm

- Japan HIV Center
  P (03) 5259-0256 **[E]**
  Saturday 1-6pm

- Japan Hotline
  P (03) 3586-0110 **[E]**

- JR (Japan Railways)
  P (03) 3423-0111 **[E]**

- Narita Flight Information
  P (0476) 34-8000, Ext. 4 for English

- NTT Directory Enquiries
  P 104 **[E]**
  Daily 9:00am-8pm

- NTT Information
  P 0120-364-463 **[E]**

- Postal Services
  P (03) 5472-5851/2 **[E]**
  Mon-Fri 9:30am-4:30pm

- Tax Counsel Office Of Tokyo Regional Taxation Bureau
  P (03) 3821-9070 **[E]**

- TELL (Tokyo English Lifeline)
  P (03) 5774-0992 **[E]** telljp.com
  Daily 9am-11pm

- Time
  P 117

- Tokyo Metro Gov't Foreign Resident Advisor
  P (03) 5320-7744
  Mon-Fri 9:30am-4pm (except 12-1)

- Visa Procedures: Extend, Change Visa Status
  P (03) 5272-4503
  Nakai Office #202 Flat Waseda
  1-9-37 Nishi-waseda, Shinjuku-ku

- Water Company
  P (03) 5320-6327 **[E]**

❖

HELPFUL WEBSITES

More helpful information about Tokyo and Japan

This chapter is to alert you to the section on the *FIT* website that contains numerous links that may be of benefit to you in your freelancing journey. The majority of sites listed are in English or have an English page. If a Japanese page is listed it's because I felt it has information or links that may not be available elsewhere. Some sites listed may seem dated, but I felt they still offered important information. For most sites a brief summary is provided so you can quickly determine if it has value for you.

As *FIT* is an ongoing project, by the time you finish reading it there may be additional categories and links on the *FIT* website. The links are active as of this writing, but if you find any that aren't, please notify me via the e-mail address listed on the *FIT* website. *FIT* is not responsible for the content or links of any of the websites listed, so proceed at your own risk.

Acronyms you should know: ELT (English Language Teacher); JLPT (Japanese Language Proficiency Test); TOEIC (Test Of English for International Communication).

The websites have been organized as follows:

Accommodations
Celebrant
Clinics/Hospitals
Coffee Shops
Computers
Concerts and Events
Department Stores
Driver's License
Earthquakes
Electronics/Appliances
Embassies
Emergencies
Employment Opportunities
Exchange Rates
Finances
Fitness
Food
Garbage
Gay & Lesbian
General
Gifts
Health Insurance
History
Honorifics
Host/Hostess
Immigration/Visas
Income Taxes
Interpretation Services

Japanese Holidays
Japanese Language Schools
Japanese Language Study
Japanese Toilets
Japlish/Engrish
Living in Japan
Love Hotels
Maps
Media
Metric Converters
Mobile Services
Narita Airport
NHK
Obatarian(s)
Office Supplies
Postal Services/UPS
Proofreader Marks
Recycling
Reference
Restaurants
Self-sponsorship
Shared Office Space
Smoking Issues
Talent Agencies
Telephone Directory
Telephone Directory
Telephone Emergencies
Temp Agency Jobs
Time Zone Converters
Tips for Teaching English
Tokyo Subways/Trains
Translation/Interpretation
Transportation
Travel
Useful Information
Ward Offices
Weather
Women
Yasukuni Shrine

CONCLUSION

Sayonara…

Must there be a conclusion to *FIT*? Not necessarily. *FIT* may lead you to a great career, lifestyle or personal relationship. But it may also lead you to realize that Japan often limits its own people by forcing them to conform—in ways that most Westerners are not comfortable with. You will find yourself "falling in line," because to get along and function here, it has to be done.

If, in fact, you start feeling that Japan is curtailing your freedom of expression or limiting your possibilities by only viewing you as a "native English speaker" or a "foreigner," it's likely that this situation will not change. On the other hand, it is exactly this situation that may provide you a lifetime of unique money-making opportunities.

That said, don't be afraid to step back after a few years and ask yourself: "Is this what I want?" Many people have a good four-to-five year run, making money, expanding cultural horizons and experiencing worlds their friends and family probably never will. But when those worlds stop spinning, don't let yourself believe that if you "stay too long" in Japan you can never return to your own country. Remember: It's your life.

For me, personally, *FIT* opened my eyes to things I never imagined I could do (film producing, screenwriting, voiceovers, etc.), not to mention helping me see myself in new ways. For these reasons and more, I am grateful. I am also grateful to the many people, mostly Japanese, who helped me when I first arrived in Tokyo. They gave me jobs, even if I didn't think I was qualified to do them. Perhaps they needed an English speaker, and one hand washed the other, so to speak. Still, they didn't have to go out of their way for me—but they did. I have no doubt you will meet similar people. I encourage you to foster relationships with them; they may last a lifetime.

So… it has come to that moment. I truly hope this book has helped you, even if you just open it now and then and say, "Oh, what happened was exactly the way he described it!" or "Thank

God he told me how to say that phrase. Now I'll get paid on time!"

Whatever your reasons for living/working in Tokyo, I hope you have a rich and fulfilling experience, and that you take that experience and reinterpret your life and dreams so that the world will become a more colorful, beautiful, fantastic place.

GLOSSARY

All the Japanese words used in FIT… and some you may encounter during your FIT experience.

aidoru アイドル
This word originally referred to young 'n cute pop "idol" singers, but now applies to any new, hot young "talent."

anime アニメ
Abbreviation for "animation."

anko あんこ
sweet red bean paste/jam (also known as *an*)

apāto アパート
An apartment, Japanese-style, with *tatami*-mat floors

bentō bako 弁当箱
lunch box

bokasu ぼかす
to shade or obscure

bōsōzoku 暴走族
Biker gangs who love to burst eardrums and burn up the black top — right outside your bedroom window at 2:00 a.m.

chikan 痴漢
molester

chousei chū 調 整 中
"Currently being repaired/adjusted" or "undergoing maintenance." Sometimes seen on monitor screens at subway/train stations instead of the usual time/station message on. Sadly, it

probably means somebody jumped onto the tracks and station personnel are busily tidying up so you can catch the next train.

chūkai tesūryou 仲介手数料
Commission received by a go-between/mediator (in this case, most likely a real estate agent)

CM シーエム
Standard abbreviation for a TV commercial

conpyūtā コンピューター
computer

cosplay コスプレ
A merging of "costume" and "role play."

dakuten 濁点
diacritic mark (゛) used to indicate "soft" voiced consonants in Japanese, i.e. the "ga" sound in *manga* would appear: まんが

dani ダニ
tick; mite

dōzo どうぞ
Please; go ahead; by all means; be my guest.

ea-kon エアコン
"air con" or air conditioner

eigo no kyōshi 英語の教師
English-language teacher (This is the phrase an English-language teacher would use to refer to himself/herself, i.e. *Watashi wa eigo no kyōshi desu.*/I am an English teacher.)

eigo no sensei 英語の先生
English-language teacher (This is the phrase that students would use to refer to an English-language teacher.)

eikaiwa 英会話
English-language conversation

enjokōsai 援助交際
"compensated dating" (prevalent between teenage girls and older men)

fudōsangyōsha 不動産業者
real estate agent/realtor

fugu ふぐ
blowfish

furigana 振り仮名
Small *hiragana* symbols written above *kanji* characters to help determine their proper readings

furikomi 振込み
A payment via bank deposit transfer

furikomu 振り込む
To make a payment via bank deposit transfer

futon 布団
Japanese bedding (roll-up mattress)

futsū 普通
General(ly), usual(ly), ordinary/ordinarily, normal

gaijin 外人
short for *gaikokujin*; foreigner (lit. outside person)

gaikokujin 外国人
foreigner

gaikokujin tōroku-shomeishō 外国人登録証明書
alien registration card

gairaigo 外来語
"borrowed" words of foreign origin

gaisensha 街宣車
Propaganda trucks. Also referred to as black sound trucks.

gaman suru 我慢する
To endure, persevere, hold up/maintain (under pressure)

gambaru/gambatte 頑張る/頑張って
To do/try one's best; to not give up (in the face of adversary)

gasu tēburu ガステーブル
one- or two-ring portable gas range/burner

giri-choko 義理チョコ
"obligatory" chocolate given to (male) bosses/co-workers by women on Valentine's Day

gomi ごみ
garbage

gyara ギャラ
Used in entertainment-related jobs. Refers to the amount of money or "guarantee" you will receive for your work.

haburashi 歯ブラシ
toothbrush

hanamizu 鼻水
(dripping) mucous (lit. nose water)

handakuten 半濁点
A diacritic mark (゜) used to indicate certain "hard" voiced consonants in the Japanese language (i.e. パン, *pan*, or "bread").

hanko 判子 (はんこ)
Seal used for signatures

henshūsha 編集者
editor (for written materials)

hiragana ひらがな
One of the three character sets used to write the Japanese language. *Hiragana* characters are written in a cursive script and are used to help clarify readings of certain *kanji* (see *furigana*), as well as for words related to grammatical functions and inflections.

hokenshō 保険証
insurance card

homū dorama ホームドラマ
television soap opera

honmei-choko 本命チョコ
"real" or "true" chocolate, given to your true love (as opposed to *giri-choko*, or "obligatory" chocolate)

Honshū 本州
One of Japan's four main islands, and the island where Tokyo is located.

hoshōnin 保証人
a guarantor/sponsor (required for any foreigner to rent an apartment or secure a work visa in Japan)

hosutesu kurabu ホステスクラブ
hostess club… where gentlemen are entertained by women who pour their drinks, light their cigarettes, etc.

irasshaimase いらっしゃいませ
Welcome!

jinji-bu 人事部
personnel department (larger than jinji-ka)

jinji-ka 人事課
personnel section

jinji-tantōsha 人事担当者
person in charge of personnel

jishin 地震
earthquake

jitensha 自転車
bicycle

jūminzei 住民税
municipal tax

ka 蚊
mosquito

kaimono 買い物
shopping

kaisha kenkō hoken 会社健康保険
employee health insurance

kanji 漢字
Multistroke characters, borrowed from the Chinese language, is one of the three character sets used to write the Japanese language.

katakana カタカナ
One of the three character sets used to write the Japanese language. *Katakana* characters are written with angular lines and are usually reserved for foreign loan words and/or for emphasis (similar to italics) in Japanese; often used in advertising.

kawaii 可愛い **(かわいい)**
cute, adorable, darling

kissaten 喫茶店
coffee/tea shop

kōban 交番
"police box"; small "offices" where policeman are available; located near major stations or busy intersections; English is rarely, if ever, spoken

koin randorī コインランドリー
Laundromat; coin laundry

kōji-chū 工事中
under construction

kokumin kenkō hoken 国民健康保険
national health insurance

konbini コンビニ
convenience store

kutsu-himo 靴紐
shoelace(s)

kuyakusho 区役所
ward/town office; the "ku" refers to the 23 wards that make up Tokyo

kyaku 客
customer or guest; usually *o-kyaku-san* or *o-kyaku-sama*

kyōshi 教師
teacher (in a classroom)

kyūkei 休憩
rest, break, intermission

LDK
Real estate acronym for Living/Dining/Kitchen. You will see: 1K (one room apartment with kitchen), 1DK (one room apartment with dining and kitchen "areas") and 1LDK (one room apartment with living, dining and kitchen "areas"). 2LDK and 3LDK can also be found (at two-three times the price).

mama-san ママさん
Usually the proprietress, owner, manager or "head hostess" of a bar or club.

manga 漫画
(Japanese-style) cartoon; comic strip

manshon マンション
(Literally: mansion) Western-style apartment; considered to be more luxurious than an *apāto* by virtue of its newness, Western-style toilet/bath, and/or hardwood floors

massāji マッサージ
massage

mata また
again, next time

meishi 名刺
business card / name card

mizu shōbai 水商売
the "water trade"; refers to club / bar nightlife

mochi 餅 /もち
Sticky rice pounded into a "cake," then steamed.

moeru gomi 燃えるごみ
burnable garbage

moenai gomi 燃えないごみ
non-burnable garbage

moshi moshi もしもし
standard telephone greeting

muryō 無料
free of charge (Sometimes used to entice customers to sign up for something or join some club.)

narētā ナレーター
narrator / voice actor

nengajō 年賀状
New Year cards

obasan おばさん
aunt or middle-aged woman

obāsan おばあさん
grandmother or elderly woman

obatarian おばたりあん
A tough middle-aged woman who could probably tackle you if you challenged her to a game of football.

o-cha お茶
(green) tea

o-chūgen お中元
mid-summer gift

ojisan おじさん
uncle or middle-aged man

ojīsan おじいさん
grandfather or elderly man

okāsan お母さん
mother

o-nigiri お握り
"rice balls" wrapped in *nori* (seaweed)

onsen 温泉
(open air) hot springs

ooya 大家
landlord

o-sechi-ryōri おせち料理
Japanese New Year's cuisine

o-seibo お歳暮
end-of-year gift

o-shibori お絞り
Small, moist towelette provided at many restaurants in Japan

otōsan お父さん
father

o-tsukaresama deshita お疲れ様 でした
(Literally: You must have been tired.) Often said as a "thank you" to someone when a job has been finished. (Sometimes used as a general greeting/goodbye in the workplace.)

o-zōni お雑煮
a hot soup that contains *mochi*, served during the New Year holiday

pachinko パチンコ
Japanese pinball game

pan パン
bread

pointo kādo ポイントカード
A point card/stamp card, usually given at supermarkets and electronic shops

rabu hoteru ラブホテル
"love" hotel

rāmen ラーメン
hot soup with noodles, vegetables and some kind of meat

randoseru ランドセル
backpack, knapsack, satchel

reikin 礼金
Commonly known as "key money." A "gift" of one or two months rent given by tenants to the landlord for the "privilege" of being allowed to live in his/her building.

reizōko 冷蔵庫
refrigerator

rōmaji ローマ字
Refers to Japanese words written in the Roman (ABC) alphabet—so us foreign folk can quickly pronounce them without spending the rest of our lives learning *kanji*.

ryokan 旅館
Japanese inn/hotel

sakka 作家
writer, author, novelist

-sama 様
a very polite suffix added to a person's name, indicative of "sir" or "madam," "Mr." or "Ms."; sometimes added to other nouns, such as *o-kyaku-sama* (honored customer/guest)

-san さん
-not as polite as *sama*; a suffix to indicate respect for who you are speaking to; even used with people you are friendly with

sararīman サラリーマン
"Salary man." A generic name for (male) company employees.

sauna サウナ
Same as it is in English.

semi 蝉
cicada

sensei 先生
(Literally: master) Used to address teachers, doctors and anyone who is considered knowledgeable.

shachō 社長
company president/manager

shikikin 敷金
security deposit

shingakujuku 進学塾
"cram" school for young students preparing for the next level of education (also known as *juku*)

shinkansen 新幹線
"bullet" (high speed) train (lit. new trunk line)

shiyakusho 市役所
municipal office/city hall

shoganai しょがない
nothing can be done; it can't/couldn't be helped

shōji 障子
sliding door with paper frames

shūten 終点
final stop; end of the line

sokutatsu 速達
Express delivery. Used at the post office to request that something be delivered the next day (within Japan).

sōpurando ソープランド
"soapland"; an establishment where men can be "bathed" or "massaged" by young women

sunakku bā スナックバー
a small bar which serves drinks and "snacks" (crackers, etc.)

sūpā スーパー
supermarket

supōtsu スポーツ
sports

taifū 台風
typhoon

takushī タクシー
taxi

tarento タレント
a catch-all word for celebrities and/or anyone who appears regularly on Japanese TV

tatami 畳
straw mats used for floor coverings

tsukemono 漬物
pickle(s)

tsuyu 梅雨
rainy season

umai 美味い
delicious, appetizing

urusai うるさい
noisy, annoying, bothersome

uyoku 右翼
right-wing

uyokudantai 右翼団体
right-wing organization

wa 和
peace, harmony

wasabi わさび
a Japanese condiment, similar to horseradish

yachin 家賃
rent (money for a house/apartment)

yōon 拗音
a diphthong

(mata) yoroshiku o-negaishimasu
（また）よろしくお願いします
Yoroshiku o-negaishimasu is really a "magic phrase" in Japanese. It basically contains the meaning of "please help/assist me", "I would really appreciate it if…", "I hope you will… think of me in the future, the next time you need my services (or I need yours)", and thoughts of this nature. Note: *Mata yoroshiku o-negaishimasu* is only used when you have *an established relationship with someone* and you are asking/hoping for his/her assistance or kindness in the future.

yūbinkyoku 郵便局
post office

zenkoku 全国
nationwide, countrywide

INDEX